SOCIOCULTURAL ORIGINS
OF ACHIEVEMENT

SOCIOCULTURAL ORIGINS OF ACHIEVEMENT

MARTIN L. MAEHR

University of Illinois

BROOKS/COLE PUBLISHING COMPANY
MONTEREY, CALIFORNIA

A Division of Wadsworth Publishing Company, Inc.

TO JANE

Without whom I might write more but enjoy it less

ISBN: 0–8185–0112–x
L.C. Catalog Card No.: 73–87051
Printed in the United States of America
1 2 3 4 5 6 7 8 9 10—78 77 76 75 74

Production Editor: Barbara Greiling
Interior & Cover Design: Linda Marcetti
Illustrations: Creative Repro, Monterey, California
Typesetting: Heffernan Press, Inc., Worcester, Massachusetts
Printing & Binding: Malloy Lithographing, Inc., Ann Arbor, Michigan

SERIES FOREWORD

The present time is an exciting period in the history of education. We are reconceptualizing the nature of formal settings in which teaching and learning take place. In addition, we are developing alternative models for teaching and learning. We have rediscovered the importance of the home, parents, and peers in the educational process. And, we are experiencing rapid change and continual advances in the technology of teaching and in the definition of the goals, objectives, and products of education.

The broad concern with the process of education has created new audiences for education-related courses, a demand for new offerings, and the need for increased flexibility in the format for courses. Furthermore, colleges and schools of education are initiating new courses and curricula that appeal to the broad range of undergraduates and that focus squarely on current and relevant social and educational issues.

The Basic Concepts in Educational Psychology series is designed to provide flexibility for both the instructor and the student. The scope of the series is broad, yet each volume in the series is self-contained and may be used as either a primary or a supplementary text. In addition, the topics for the volumes in the series have been carefully chosen so that several books in the series may be adopted for use in introductory courses or in courses with a more specialized focus. Furthermore, each of the volumes is suitable for use in classes operating on the semester or quarter system, or for modular, in-service training, or workshop modes of instruction.

Larry R. Goulet

PREFACE

A child is not born into a social vacuum; neither is he unresponsive to experience. Therefore, social and cultural factors affect whatever he is or becomes. This book is concerned with those social events, institutions, and experiences that fill up the psychological space in which the child exists. It is most pointedly concerned with how these social and cultural factors shape his capacity and his will to achieve. Thus, the book is written for those who have a broad and general interest in education—for teacher candidates, administrators, teachers, and, hopefully, certain lay persons.

This book focuses on such questions as: How does social background affect intellectual development? What social and cultural factors condition achievement motivation? Why don't children from certain backgrounds do well in school? Although such questions are discussed in undergraduate courses in education, psychology, and sociology, few relevant textual sources that relate to them are currently available. A concerted attempt has been made to deal with problem areas as the practitioner confronts them rather than as they are conceptualized by the scholar. For this reason, major attention is given to "motivational questions" and to questions of teacher influence and expectancy. While a brief volume such as this is necessarily limited in its scope and coverage, the reader should nevertheless gain a clear picture of the problems and possibilities involved in educating children of diverse sociocultural origins. That, at least, is my fond hope.

Although writing is a lonely task, it is not pursued in complete isolation. I am indebted in many ways to my friend and colleague Larry R. Goulet of the University of Illinois, who not only asked me to write this book but also encouraged me to complete it. Professor Goulet, along with William Stallings of Georgia State University, Douglas Sjogren of Colorado State University, Paul Torrance of the University of Georgia, and Howard Rollins of Emory University, provided criticism and suggestions that were of major help.

It was in the context of my involvement with the University of

Illinois Committee on Culture and Education that many of my ideas about culture and human development were developed, tested, and improved. All the members of that group deserve my thanks, but I am particularly grateful to Professor Jacquetta Burnett, who as an anthropologist, repeatedly reminded me of my psychological bias. Finally, I am especially indebted to my students, whose enthusiasm encouraged me to believe that this area of study is indeed significant, and to my wife, Jane, who reminded me that writing books is not *all* there is to life.

Martin L. Maehr

CONTENTS

CHAPTER FIVE

PERSON, SITUATION, AND ACHIEVEMENT   64

CHAPTER SIX

A CONCLUDING CAVEAT   82

SOCIOCULTURAL ORIGINS OF ACHIEVEMENT

CHAPTER
ONE
INTRODUCTION

In 1954 the U. S. Supreme Court heard the case of *Brown* vs. *Board of Education of Topeka*. The issue was whether educating the races separately results in educating them unequally. In making its ruling, the court rejected the "separate but equal" tradition and declared segregated schooling unlawful. This decision led to more than a change in legal opinion; it unleashed a powerful force for social change throughout the United States. Some of the most immediate effects were felt in the schools. With the integration of a Little Rock, Ark., high school, the color and possibly the character of American education began to change slowly but perceptibly. Blacks entered previously all-white schools, and officially segregated school systems began to disappear under court order, legislative encouragement, and government programs. The United States and its schools had started on a new venture. Problems of severe cultural difference and deprivation were to be confronted head-on and, hopefully, solved.

In 1964 Congress passed a civil rights act that involved further restructuring of society to break down cultural barriers against minority groups. With this legislation, provision was made to evaluate the progress made thus far. The result was one of the largest social-science research projects in history, the Coleman Report (1966).[1]

The academic progress of over 500,000 pupils was assessed and related to information about their teachers, schools, and homes. Schools from each region of the country, students representing different social and cultural contexts in the United States, and teachers of varying competence, experience, and maturity were systematically studied to determine what "made a difference" in achievement. Of course, there was a special concern to see whether the goals implicit in the 1954 court decision had in any sense been realized.

[1] The report was submitted to the President as a report on *Equality of Educational Opportunity*. Since a sociologist by the name of James Coleman headed the research team that prepared the report, the document is typically referred to as the "Coleman Report."

The findings were not only interesting but downright provocative. To some they were disturbing, if not shocking. The report documented what many had already suspected—that is, that children from minority groups performed at a lower level than children from the white majority. The typical black, Mexican, Puerto Rican, or American Indian child began school with a clear achievement disadvantage. That is, he entered school with less preparation and, predictably enough, initially exhibited a poor performance pattern. Moreover, this clear difference in performance persisted throughout the child's schooling experience.

Initial differences in school achievement were not altogether surprising. After all, a raft of preschool programs had already been established to do something about this problem. However, the fact that such differences persisted throughout the schooling experience was a disturbing discovery. Apparently, the schools and education programs were not closing the gap. The belief that schools could be instruments of social change received a severe blow. Furthermore, the report gave little or no comfort to those who assumed that ending the schools' failure in this regard was only a matter of improving the facilities, the quality of teachers, or the design of curriculum. The Coleman Report took specific note of the fact that variations in these educational inputs seemed to make little or no difference in the quality of outputs. The final blow was that school integration itself was not found to be a dynamic positive force in equalizing achievement among cultural groups. The winning argument in *Brown* vs. *Board of Education of Topeka* seemed less persuasive in 1966 than it did in 1954. The Coleman Report and other data indicated that integration might help—*somewhat*. But there was no decisive evidence on which to argue that integration would create equality of educational opportunity and close cultural gaps in achievement. Integration by itself was definitely *not* the answer in solving the race- and/or culture-related problems of school achievement. In fact, from the Coleman Report, there seemed to be no answer of major value associated with the schools.

The myth of the schools as instruments of social change was severely shaken, but the importance of sociocultural factors in creating and controlling achievement was highlighted. Certainly the early attempts to use the school to do away with so-called cultural deprivation or social disadvantage prompted, at the very least, a recognition that social and cultural factors were important. The Coleman Report and the discussion that it prompted (Mosteller & Moynihan, 1972; Jencks et al., 1972) may have increased our recognition of the nature and importance of cultural differences. As it questioned whether educational institutions could effectively deal with cultural differences in achievement, the report suggested that economics, home background, peer experiences, and a host of other extraschool experiences should be the objects of focus. In effect, it said that education as it occurs naturally and informally in various social and cultural groups must be considered if we are to begin to understand the phenomenon of achievement.

Today's data may raise serious questions about yesterday's policies and even shake our beliefs in schooling itself. However, the tortuous path of educational change followed by the schools since 1954 highlights an issue of persisting concern—namely, that education does not occur in a social and cultural vacuum and that students cannot be viewed apart from the context in which they were born and raised and in which they spend the major portion of their time.

Achievement is related to the sociocultural origin of the student and to the sociocultural context in which he is educated. The plaintiffs in *Brown* vs. *Board of Education of Topeka* were obviously cognizant of this fact. The Coleman Report documented on a grand scale just how important and pervasive these differences are. It also added one other critical insight. By exhibiting the schools' incapacity for ameliorating differences in achievement among social and cultural groups, it called attention to the wider social and cultural context in which teaching and learning occur. Teachers cannot ignore the social and cultural background of the child. The home is critical in the educational process, and what happens outside the school grounds is equally if not more important than what happens within.

In short, the events of the 1950s and 1960s have made it necessary for us to give serious consideration to the *sociocultural origins of achievement*. And that, of course, is the topic of this book. The book will not solve the problems that *Brown* vs. *Board of Education of Topeka* and the Coleman Report have left unsolved. Neither will it answer the questions that they have raised. What it will do, I hope, is make educators poignantly aware of cultural differences—particularly of those differences that affect teaching, learning, and achievement.

THE NATURE OF ACHIEVEMENT

But what is *achievement*? In the Coleman Report, as well as for many educators, achievement is primarily *verbal* achievement—that is, the performance that can be readily assessed by means of standardized tests. Even when the definition of achievement goes beyond verbal performance to include such things as mechanical, clerical, and problem-solving skills, we have a feeling of uneasiness. Certainly, this is not *all* that there is to achievement. What about the ability to organize and lead demonstrated by a Cesar Chavez? What about the accomplishments of a Bob Gibson or achievements of a Johnny Carson or Isaac Stern? Quite clearly, any conception of achievement must encompass such activities as well as course grades and scores on standardized tests. Is there any common element in all these activities that might serve as an acceptable working definition of achievement?

Achievement is commonly associated with some type of *performance*. Something measurable has to be done or accomplished. However, the term "achievement" is not applied to *every* activity that is measurable. Cracking your knuckles or scratching your ear is not usually considered an achievement. Rather, the term is reserved for those instances in which some *standard of excellence* is applied to the situation. Of course, the judgment of excellence may be in terms of the individual's own accomplishments or in terms of a group norm of some kind. But whatever the standard, the point is that the *quality* of performance is or can be evaluated.

Also implicit in the discussion thus far is the idea that achievement involves some *uncertainty in outcome*. When there is no doubt as to the outcome of an activity, it is typically thought of as habitual. We usually reserve the term "achievement" to refer to some sort of activity in which the outcome is not habitual or inevitable.

Finally, achievement is something done *by* a person, not something done *for* him. When a performance or an accomplishment is attributed to an individual—when he, personally, is responsible for the result—then, and usually only then, do we speak of achievement.

Thus, achievement may be appropriately defined as (1) a measurable change in behavior (2) attributed to some person as the causal agent (3) that is or can be evaluated in terms of a standard of excellence and (4) that typically involves some uncertainty as to the outcome or quality of the accomplishment.

Although everything that has been said obviously applies to school achievement, it does not necessarily stop there. Achievement embraces many facets of life other than reading, writing, arithmetic, and other activities to which we typically assign grades. It can, and indeed should, embrace athletic accomplishments, musical performance, business enterprise, and many other areas of activity. After all, achievement and learning do occur outside the classroom.

SOCIOCULTURAL INFLUENCES ON ACHIEVEMENT

This book is concerned with questions like the following: Why do some people achieve more or at a higher level than others? Why do some situations prompt increased accomplishments while others do not? How can people be motivated? How can achievement be increased? In answering these questions, the book will focus on social and cultural factors. How do cultures, social groups, and situations mold achievement patterns?

SOCIAL EXPERIENCE AND HUMAN DEVELOPMENT

In order to provide some context for answering such questions, we will consider briefly the role of social experience in human development.

Let us begin *near* the beginning. At birth, the child seems scarcely human. He is hardly aware of his surroundings. Primarily struggling for existence, he is responsive only to his needs, wants, pleasures, and pains. But as helpless and unresponsive as the newborn may seem, it soon becomes obvious that an amazing potential is built into this little package. After a few weeks, the infant begins to exhibit a measure of control over some of his movements. Gradually, he seems to break out of his world and show some surprising capacities. Not only does he begin to exhibit an ever-increasing responsiveness to others, but he begins to do things, to accomplish tasks, and to achieve.

At the basis of this development there are, of course, inherited predispositions. Genetic inheritance determines or affects certain "physical" traits—the shape of the nose, the rate of growth, the size of the head. It also appears to strongly influence so-called psychological traits. For example, intelligence, or the capacity to learn and benefit from experience, is at least in part a function of hereditary predispositions. Because he is human, the child will exhibit a specifiable course of intellectual development; because he is the recipient of a certain genetic heritage, he will likely exhibit greater or lesser intellectual capacity.

But genetic predispositions alone do not determine the course of development; neither is behavioral potential irrevocably set at conception. To a considerable extent a person is what he is as the result of the experiences he has had. People *learn* to be what they are. This is particularly true in the case of socially oriented behavior, or in those aspects of our lives that seem most clearly *human*. Take, for example, the phenomenon of self-regard. Each of us has developed some basic notions about what and who we are, about what we can and cannot do, and about our goodness and badness as persons. To think about ourselves in these ways is most thoroughly human. Perhaps it is even the prime distinguishing human characteristic, as philosophical and theological discussions have often implied. How does this critical aspect of our humanity emerge and evolve?

The capacity to reflect in such ways seems quite clearly to be genetic—that is, a sheer function of being human. However, the *way* we come to think about ourselves is a function of experience—most particularly of social experience. That is, it is formed by the responses of others to us. Thus, when parents approve, disapprove, encourage, or restrain, they not only affect the behavior of the moment but may also create in the child a certain image of himself that affects his continuing interests, aspirations, and desires. Teachers may also perform similar functions, and their influence is, in many cases, no less pervasive. A series of studies (Haas & Maehr, 1965; Ludwig & Maehr, 1967; Maehr, Nafzger, & Mensing, 1962) on the development of self-esteem has made this point inescapably clear. In these studies, adolescent boys were asked to perform various physical tasks in the presence of a "physical-development expert." Following their performance, they were randomly given either a positive or a negative evaluation—that is, they were told that they did or did not demonstrate the physical skill appropriate for a person of their age. Although this encounter with a significant other was brief, its effects were powerful. With little or no apparent resistance, these boys subsequently evaluated themselves as they had been evaluated. Even more surprising—indeed, disturbing—was how readily this evaluation of one small aspect of their self seemed to affect not only general self-esteem but also motivation. Subsequent tests of interest revealed that positive or negative evaluation was directly related to continued inclination to engage in physical or athletic activities. Apparently, even momentary social encounters can drastically influence the child's view of himself. Furthermore, as his self-image is changed, so are the form and direction of his behavior. Individuals most often do not attempt what they do not think they can do. When forced to work in those areas in which they have low self-esteem, they are typically less than enthusiastic.

But all of this is not particularly surprising. These studies only seem to specify, clarify, and perhaps enhance what, in a general way, should be obvious to each of us. Persons who are important to us do affect the way we define ourselves. Think back on your life, and you can probably verify this. One teacher's approval made you "realize" you could become a good student, while an indication of disapproval may have discouraged your interest in another area. The fact that you are in college is not only a function of your IQ; it is also a product of the fact that parents, teachers, and peers communicated to you that you could and should go to college. Probably the social context in which you grew up defined you as "college bound," and perhaps you have never questioned this definition of yourself.

The fact that this experience is commonplace and perhaps obvious does not diminish its importance. Furthermore, it is possible that certain evaluative responses may be inherent within particular social contexts in which a child may be placed or may find himself. That is, the significant others within these situations may be predisposed to evaluate a child positively or negatively and thus increase or decrease his self-regard. Consider the child who grows up as a member of a disadvantaged minority group. His experience throughout much of his life is similar to that of the disapproval group in the experimental studies just reviewed. If he is black, it is possible that in a white-dominant society he comes to associate the very color of his skin with badness, incompetence, and worthlessness. Not only does blackness identify him with a minority group that is often rejected, but it also serves as a stimulus to teachers, shopkeepers, and policemen to treat him in a negative fashion (see Coates, 1972; Rubovits & Maehr, 1971, in preparation). It is not surprising, then, that the black child growing up in a white society often rejects his ethnic identification and sometimes views his very blackness negatively. In a classic study Clark and Clark (1947) showed black and white dolls to 7-year-old black children and asked them such questions as "which doll looks nice?" "which doll looks bad?" and "which doll is a 'nice' color?" Most of these black children indicated that it was the white doll that "looked nice" and had a "nice color" and the black doll that "looked bad." More recent studies of this type (see Asher & Allen, 1969; Coles, 1965; Proshansky & Newton, 1968, p. 186 f.) have generally supported the notion that black children do evaluate themselves and even their color negatively. However, there is at least some reason to hope that attempts to emphasize that "black is beautiful" eventually will change the situation (Lessing & Zagorin, 1972a, 1972b).

Whether or not a person is black, the fact that he is from an impoverished stratum of society seems to place him in a position in which his attempts to achieve are almost inevitably met with failure. It is not that such a person hasn't tried. It is not that he has totally rejected the values of the wider culture. Rather, as Liebow (1967) points out in his study of "street-corner men," such a person has tried and repeatedly failed. He experiences this failure in the world of work and again when he returns to a family setting. His marriage is probably not a success, and his family life does not provide much support for his self-esteem. Except in the company of fellow failures, he experiences little self-approval and little acknowledgment that he has the competence to succeed at anything. His life is a series of disapproval experiences that can only result in negative self-esteem and a subsequent tendency to quit trying.

What can and obviously does happen in the area of self-regard is a profound example of how social experiences affect the course of human development. There are, of course, other examples. As this book will point out, social experience changes not only beliefs, attitudes, and thoughts but perhaps the very capacity to think. To a surprising degree, we are each a product of the social context into which we were born, in which we were raised, and in which we now live.

SOCIAL CONTEXT AND BEHAVIOR

Each person has a social past as well as a social present. What happens now is a product of both our several backgrounds *and* an immediate social context.

An immediate social context may vary in a number of ways. Social contexts may contain different kinds of people. A grouping of individuals with similar backgrounds will inevitably vary from one in which each individual is from a different culture. That much is obvious. In addition, factors such as group size, assigned task, operational rules, and goals will inevitably affect a social context regardless of the backgrounds of the participants. Thus in one classroom, or learning group, there may be multiple goals and varied tasks, and the students may choose what they want to do when they want to do it. In another, a group task may be followed by individual tasks—all assigned by a teacher. Obviously, a learning group, as well as any social group, can be arranged in a variety of ways. Such arrangements may create qualitatively different psychological climates—climates that are variously characterized as open, free, humane, teacher-centered, repressive, and so on.

That the effects of such climates may be broad and pervasive is evident from a number of different studies of group climate. In one series of studies, for example, it has been customary to distinguish between *democratic* and *authoritarian* climates. In the authoritarian climate, the leader or teacher dominates the decision making. In the democratic climate, group members participate actively in deciding on group goals and tasks. The effects of the different climates are often profound. In the now-classic study by White and Lippitt (1968), an authoritarian climate bred dependence on the leader. The behavior of the group members as well as the whole pattern of group activity reflected this dependence. When the leader left the room, the authoritarian group was much more likely to break off work than the democratic group was. In addition, boys moving from an authoritarian to a more permissive climate produced an outburst of raucous activity. Perhaps they needed to "blow off steam" after being oppressed for a while, or perhaps they had not developed personal social controls. Whatever the precise reason, it seems clear that the industrious behavior of authoritarian groups was strongly tied to the presence of the leader.

However, while authoritarianism resulted in considerable productivity, there was a different spirit involved. The boys not only preferred the democratic groups, but they seemed to work as efficiently and possibly more creatively in them. Above all, the whole affective climate was quite different in the two groups. There was more hostile and aggressive activity in the authoritarian groups than in the democratic groups. In general, the democratic groups were characterized by a spirit of cooperation and friendliness.

It is tempting to oversimplify and to say that a democratic climate has a "good" effect and an authoritarian climate has a "bad" effect. However, another group climate was also considered by White and Lippitt: a *laissez faire* group. In this group, the leader allowed the students to do whatever they wanted with little or no direction or intervention. This group climate was the least effective and desirable from almost any perspective. It was really the "bad" group.

The Lippitt and White study emphasizes the importance of the immediate social context. Certainly, this and a host of other studies have indicated that we cannot ignore the present social scene. A person's behavior of the moment is not just a product of his earlier experiences—that is, how he was treated by parents and what he was taught to think, believe, and value; it is also a product of the contemporary and even immediate social situation—that is, of the behavior of his teacher and peers; of his opportunities to do, be, or become, and of rewards, punishments, and rules he is given. Both the past and the present are important. A teacher had better hope that this is true!

PRESENT AND PAST SOCIAL EXPERIENCE

How do past and present interact? It is interesting and rewarding to search out the effects of past experiences and present social context separately. But it is especially intriguing to consider how persons from different backgrounds may respond to varying social contexts. It is more than interesting and intriguing—it is critical! If you were to visit a classroom in Iran, you would see children reciting or taking dictation, almost always sitting or standing with face toward teacher. The teacher is in control, and the children accept the guidelines that he or she establishes—make no mistake about that. Moreover, the educational process seems to function rather well despite an authoritarianism and rigidity that would be shunned by the most domineering of American teachers. What would happen if these same children were placed in a highly flexible, open, free, and *democratic* school environment? Would the background of these students, the culture that is associated with Iranian village life, doom such an experiment to failure? There is an example closer to home. Teachers in the inner city contend that it is impossible to establish rules, manage a classroom, or reward behavior in the same way there as in the suburbs. Perhaps they are right. But in what way are they right? How might a learning environment be structured to best match the predispositions of a child from this or that inner-city or suburban background? This question gets to the heart of the matter and, in an important sense, to the heart of this book.

A LOOK AHEAD

This book is concerned with describing the social and cultural factors that make a difference as far as achievement is concerned. Although the majority of readers will likely be most concerned with social and cultural variations that they might experience in the United States, an interest in the effects of such variations often prompts us to look beyond our own borders. If our only standards for assessing the nature of family life are those derived from predominant American patterns, we may easily view the ghetto family as disorganized, disintegrated, and a clear case of deterioration from the ideal. A knowledge of family life in a broad range of cultures, however, may at the very least cause us to be less rigid in our judgments as we recognize patterns that also exist elsewhere—and successfully so (see Valentine, 1968). In any case, don't be surprised when I "take" you to Iran, Africa, or Russia to provide perspective on a situation confronting the American child or the American school. After all, we are interested in how social experiences, wherever they might exist, can affect behavior.

But the book is quite obviously not only concerned with the nature of social and cultural variation. It is specifically and emphatically concerned with how such variation makes a difference as far as achievement is concerned. How does or how might the experience of living in a toyless, bookless, and teacherless home affect one's very capacity to learn? How does being black in a white world or poor in an affluent society affect the will to achieve? How does one go about coping with children of diverse backgrounds? How do the teacher's social origins affect his behavior toward students? These are the kinds of questions that prompted me to write this book. Not all of them will be answered to everyone's satisfaction. But perhaps an occasional insight will be precipitated, a new perspective provided, or a productive line of questioning suggested.

CHAPTER
TWO
CULTURE, CLASS, GROUP, AND PERSON

World travelers as well as sixth-graders know that there is something different about people and their behavior in Alaska, Algeria, Australia, and the Azores. Neither a sixth-grader nor a world traveler is necessarily able to specify these differences—but they know they are there. Similarly, the typical Headstart teacher knows that her charges do not fully participate in the same social world that she does—even if she seems a bit incoherent in describing either their world or her world. It is interesting simply to survey the multiplicity of human differences that exist across nations, societies, and groups. That, I suppose, is one reason why *National Geographic* continues to be popular.

But the purpose of this chapter is not to provide a catalog of cultural and societal differences—indeed, that would be impossible. Rather, its purpose is to define a bit more precisely the nature of social contexts. How might they be characterized? How are they likely to vary? How will such variations make a difference in the person? Thus far, terms like "class" and "culture" have been used in a rather general way to describe readily recognizable and understandable situations. Now it is time to be a bit more specific.

CULTURE

The concept "culture" is basic to our concern here. Having defined it, we will have gone a significant distance in identifying those facets of social experience that affect achievement. Before discussing culture, however, it is necessary to take note of a critical characteristic of man as a social creature—that is, the tendency for individuals to conform to group norms. Indeed, our understanding of culture is dependent upon an understanding of this apparent *sine qua non* of human nature.

NORMS AND CONFORMITY

When people, be they children or adults, are placed in a situation in which they must behave with reference to one another, interesting things happen. After a while, their behavior follows certain predictable patterns. Rules, regulations, customs, and styles emerge, and everyone is obliged to give recognition if not subservience to them. In other words, social *norms* evolve. A first and basic principle of social interaction concerns the emergence of such standards for behavior.

Whenever two or more people behave in concert, a standard of behavior is either implicitly or explicitly formulated, and the behavior of the individuals involved tends increasingly to converge on this standard. In an early and now-classic study on this point, Sherif (1935, 1936) provided a clear example of the emergence of norms and normative behavior. His study exhibits what happens at some point in most social groups. It also demonstrates phenomena that are basic to such complex entities as social institutions, societies, and cultures. Sherif arranged for groups of individuals to view a small, stationary spot of light in an otherwise completely darkened room. When a light is viewed under these conditions, it appears to move. This movement illusion is technically referred to as the *autokinetic* effect. Sherif was not, of course, interested in the illusion per se. Rather, his concern revolved around the question of *how much* movement the subjects would attribute to the spot of light.

Although he expected a great deal of individual variation to begin with, he predicted that eventually the judgments made by the group members would converge on some standard. That is, after some period of time, the members would begin to agree on how much the light moved. Convergence on a group standard did occur. Although there was presumably no external pressure to do so, the subjects eventually tended to exhibit agreement regarding this subjective experience. Furthermore, the subjects apparently were quite unaware that they were establishing a group standard. As far as they were concerned, they were simply reporting events as they occurred. It is especially interesting to note that norms arrived at in this manner tend to outlive the immediate context and to have continuing influences on the members of the group. Sherif found that, when a group member was later asked to judge the movement of the light in isolation from the group, he reported movement that approximated the group norm. The group provided "truth" in an ambiguous situation; that truth remained as an abiding principle for the individual even after the group no longer existed.

The fact that norms emerge is important. What is equally important, however, is the tendency for groups to exact or to be granted conformity once a norm does arise. Sherif found that subjects who had initially made judgments in isolation changed their judgments in accord with an established group norm when they subsequently joined an ongoing group. That is, even though they had already established their own answers to the problem of wandering lights, they nevertheless adapted their answers to group truth when they became members of the group.

The power of the group to influence the individual is nowhere more clearly illustrated than in studies conducted by Asch (1952, 1958). His goal was to determine whether or not the standard of the group would be sufficiently powerful in some circumstances to force the individual to deny his own sensory experience. Asch arranged for each individual to make various judgments regarding the length of lines. From the judgments made by a control group, it was clear that this task could be done with minimal error and considerable ease. However, each of Asch's experimental subjects made their judgments as participants in a group—a group in which the other members were confederates of the experimenter with the specific assignment of making erroneous judgments on certain tasks. What happened in this situation is extremely fascinating to the social scientist, although it was rather disconcerting to the naive subject. Each naive subject placed in this situation exhibited some effects of group pressure. Most of them conformed, denied their senses, and went along with the group error. Some appeared to conform with little or no insight into what they were doing; others conformed verbally but later expressed reservations about what they were doing. Only a few "called them as they saw them," and even they did so with difficulty. That is, it seemed almost traumatic for the subjects not to follow the group even when it was "obvious" that the group was wrong.

Groups create norms, and individuals, within limits, conform. However, norms often outlive the people and conditions that were initially responsible for their existence. An interesting capstone to both the Sherif and the Asch studies is a study by Jacobs and Campbell (1961) in which the development and transmission of norms over a number of "generations" were observed. As in the Sherif studies, various groups viewed a stationary light in a darkened room and made judgments regarding the amount of movement. Jacobs and Campbell, however, also borrowed a page from Asch's book and arranged it so that at the first session a majority of each viewing group were in fact confederates. The task of these confederates was to create an arbitrary movement norm by their responses. This arbitrary norm was designed to be more extreme than was usually found in studies on the autokinetic effect. Thus, it was possible to determine if subjects were conforming to the imposed norm or if they were simply expressing other inclinations. (There does seem to be a "natural range" within which the perception of movement is typically limited.)

In view of Asch's work, it is not surprising that Jacobs and Campbell's confederates were able to establish a predetermined arbitrary norm for the minority. What is most fascinating is that this norm, once established, outlived the presence of the confederates. During the course of the experiment, the confederates were systematically removed from each viewing group and replaced with naive subjects. Thus, a majority of confederates became a minority, and, finally, the groups were entirely composed of naive subjects. Interestingly enough, the norms initially established by the confederates persisted, on the average, for four or five generations beyond the last confederate. Naive subjects were passing along the normative tradition they had received instead of responding independently and situationally to the immediate task. In short, the Jacobs and Campbell study provides an example not only of conformity to a group norm but also of the transmission of a tradition and conformity to it.

The emergence of norms, the pressures for conformity, and the transmission of normative traditions are very familiar facets of life. All of us have experienced something like the Sherif, Asch, and Jacobs and Campbell situations—only for real. To be human is to participate in groups, and group participation inevitably involves conformity to norms.

An obvious and major reason for the variation in individual behavior is group membership. Sam from the ghetto and Johnny from suburbia are different because they participate in different groups and conform to different norms. Similarly, the behavior of people around the world is extremely varied simply because they hold membership in groups that have evolved separately and thus have produced their own traditions and standards of reference. The behavior of any given individual is largely explainable in terms of his attempt to conform to the groups that are significant to him. After all, if he does not conform, he can expect some kind of group sanction. But there is also the fact that, when experienced reality is ambiguous, social reality (the group's prescription) may be the best guide.

CULTURE AS A COMPLEX OF NORMS

To a considerable extent, a "culture" consists of the norms, guidelines, and prescriptions that any given group of individuals holds in common. When we talk of the cultural origins of Sonny Suburb or George Ghetto, we are talking about a complex of norms extant for an identifiable, interdependent group in which that individual holds membership. The use of the term "culture" assumes that such a group of individuals has been functioning in an interdependent fashion over a period of time. Given such conditions, there will be normative products. These normative products are a critical if not *the* critical feature of a culture. Of course, in most natural-istic settings, the norms will not revolve primarily around wandering lights. They will be shared answers to questions that concern the group, answers to questions regarding how life is to be lived, answers that outlive the immediate context of their origins, and answers that, to a greater or lesser degree, are imposed on new members as they join the group.

Normative Questions

Saying that culture is a set of norms or guidelines that characterizes a group and influences the individuals who belong to that group is not enough. In order to see how cultures can vary, we must consider the kind of normative questions that human experience forces us to ask and the variety of answers that can be given.[1]

Structuring the world.   There are several different kinds of norma-tive questions that seem to be universal, although the answers vary widely across groups. Among these universal questions are those related to pro-viding a structure for the world that we experience through our senses. You don't need a course in psychology to know that there is often a big dif-ference between what *is* and what we *see*. Each person is confronted with a bewildering array of stimuli, and the sheer enormity and complexity of stimulation force him to attend to certain things and not to others. In addition, patterns of stimulation are often open to a variety of perceptual interpretations. Two persons looking at an inkblot rarely see the same thing. Many day-to-day happenings are similarly ambiguous and open to different interpretations. Within groups, however, regularities emerge in relation to these ambiguous perceptual phenomena. Thus, as will be dis-cussed in Chapter Three, individuals who have grown up in different so-cieties will probably follow different guidelines in selecting and interpreting sensory experience. That is, they will perceive different worlds.

Explaining events.   There are also normative questions of cause and effect. In each individual's experience, events occur that demand expla-nation, and, within each cultural group, there exists a preferred explanation. Consider the example of a young American child who suddenly becomes seriously ill. He would be taken to a hospital and seen by specialists who speak vaguely of "viruses" of an unknown source and nature. The shared

---

[1] The normative questions identified here were developed along lines sug-gested by Goodenough (1963, p. 258 *ff.*; 1971).

belief of both parents and specialists is that the cause is physical, within the realm of the natural, and ultimately controllable by physical treatment. In a "primitive" or less "advanced" society, a child might also be brought to a specialist. However, the belief system there, as well as much of the behavior, would clearly be different. The talk might possibly be of demons or of magic spells and the treatment spiritual rather than physical. In either case, and in spite of the treatment perhaps, the child might recover, and, thus, the belief systems would be reinforced. Two different cultures may have two different ways of interpreting the same "facts." Cause and effect often are conceptualized quite differently across cultures.

Choosing, striving, and aspiring. Besides guidelines for perceiving and explaining, a culture is characterized by the way in which its members organize, identify, and select purposes and preferences. In other words, value systems, an ideology, and life goals are critical features of any culture. In this regard, it is helpful to turn to the work of Florence Kluckhohn (Kluckhohn, 1961; Kluckhohn & Strodtbeck, 1961). She has suggested that life style is significantly determined by the answers that persons and groups give to five basic questions.

1. The first question is concerned with *man's relationship to other men.* Is the relationship individualistic, with great stress placed on the *individual's* accomplishments, personal rights, and personal freedoms? Is the relationship "collateral," with the extended family, the community, or the tribe in a position of primacy? Or is it "lineal," with the group, as it extends through time and across generations, primary? Even a cursory review of the anthropological literature makes it clear that the relationship of man to man is subject to significant variation. Moreover, the nature of this relationship will inevitably affect the nature of achievement valued by a group. A classroom activity that involves the individual student in competition with his fellow students may work well within a culture in which an individualistic ethic is adhered to but may fail miserably within another culture. The Navajo child, in contrast to the child from Shaker Heights, is not likely to respond as favorably to motivational appeals associated with competitive-grading procedures. He comes from a cultural background that does not value individual achievement as highly as it does a harmonious, cooperative relationship among members.

2. A second question concerns *time.* Groups and persons can be differentiated by the emphasis they place on the present, past, and future. The schools that I attended were primarily future-oriented institutions: places where students were *prepared for life.* For good or ill, most of what was said and done was justified on the basis of future concerns. We learned arithmetic because someday we would need to make change, compute

income tax, design computers, or simply do the next level of math. Such an emphasis on the future was shared by those who had a significant interest in the schools, and I was in fact surrounded by people, institutions, and events that focused on tomorrow rather than on today or yesterday. However, not all people or cultural groups tie their lives so closely to the future. No one has made this point more adequately than Oscar Lewis in *Children of Sanchez* (1961). A first-person account of the Sanchez family, the book poignantly describes belief systems characteristic of many cultural groups. In this Mexican family, the time notion was completely different from that of futuristically inclined middle-class Americans. Either implicitly or explicitly, the dialogue affirms that the significant time was the *present*. This family and their compatriots did not typically save what little income they received in order to purchase desirables sometime in the future. They did not lay up a store for future bad times. Their belief, continually reinforced by cold fact, was that denying oneself now would have little or no effect on future happiness.

3. A third question that Kluckhohn suggests is "what is the *valued personality type?*" Different social groups value and promote different modal patterns. Whereas spending the day whittling wood may be an acceptable mode for one group, contemplation and meditation may be desirable in a second group, and a third group may espouse activity, or "busy-ness," even for its own sake. It is difficult for many of us to understand the importance placed on meditation and contemplation among medieval monks or oriental holy men. I am told that American businessmen scurrying about Rome, Tehran, or Delhi are equally inscrutable.

4. Perhaps our predilection for being, becoming, and doing is at least partially related to a fourth question: "what is the relationship of man to nature?" Is man subjected to nature? Is man seen as existing "in nature"? Or is it man "over nature"? The Bible of Jews and Christians suggests (Genesis 1:28) that man is to conquer and subdue the earth. Subsequently, Western science and technology have proceeded to do just that—sometimes with fearful side effects. However, the typical Spanish-American sheepraiser of the Southwest was not, at least a generation or so ago, inclined to believe that much could be done to protect his "business" from natural catastrophes or to guard himself from personal tragedy. Storms and illness were solely matters of "God's will," and there was little point in trying to prevent their occurrence or counteract their effects. The concept of man as integral within nature or actually dominated by nature is probably not conducive to the growth of technology. However, it may be conducive to the preservation of nature and the conservation of natural resources, as is evidenced by certain American Indian cultures.

5. Finally, each group must answer the question "what are the

innate predispositions of man?" Evil? Neither good nor bad? Good? In any case, can these predispositions be changed? And if so, to what can man be changed? We don't have to compare "advanced" with "primitive" cultures or East with West to be aware of the interesting variations that occur. I have always been amused at the variety of opinions that I can find on this point in my own neighborhood. But of course, the issue here is that cultural groups do differ in important ways regarding the predispositions of man. The stand they take on this question is necessarily a critical facet of their culture.

Kluckhohn's work nicely illustrates how men and cultural groups may vary with regard to life style. The variables that are identifiable in terms of these five questions, however, are not all-inclusive. Although they adequately summarize the ways in which preferences are organized, they possibly slight the organization of purposes. These questions deal with what might be called "instrumental values"—that is, with preferred ways of accomplishing things. People also differ in terms of "terminal values" or life goals. Within our own society, such goals as salvation, freedom, and justice are rather clearly articulated. Moreover, whether we view salvation as more important than happiness or freedom as more important than justice is crucial to the style of life we exhibit. As children are taught to do things in certain ways or to *be* according to certain modes, they are also taught to work toward certain ends. What ends will be promoted is a variable feature of cultural groups. Thus, Rokeach (1968, p. 170 *ff.*) found preference for certain terminal values to vary markedly among groups of diverse backgrounds. While a group of unemployed blacks rated "equality" first and "freedom" tenth on a list of 12 terminal values, other groups, such as unemployed whites or students at a Calvinist college, exhibited drastically different preferences. Most intriguing is a comparison of unemployed blacks with their oftimes antagonists from a counterculture, policemen. Preferences of these two groups were in sharp contrast on the terminal values of "freedom" and "equality." The policemen ranked "freedom" first and "equality" twelfth.

Doing.   Finally, a culture consists significantly, and sometimes most obviously, of a set of guidelines for "doing." Life has to be organized in such a way that certain basic human needs are met. The way in which a group has organized itself to meet these needs and the recipes it has for action are significant aspects of its culture. The necessity for food and warmth is universal, but *what* we eat and *how* we dress are matters of cultural determination as well as necessity. When a person is born into a given social group, he is provided with a set of ready-made, tried, and possibly true answers to some of these basic questions of survival. Because a person is born into a Masai tribe in Africa, he will cherish blood from a living cow rather than steak from a dead one. Because he is born, raised, and lives out his life in Suburbia, U. S. A., another person will prefer a Hart, Shaffner, and Marx creation to a loincloth, at least for the working hours.

Associated with such ways of handling basic needs are techniques and a technology. There are techniques that each group of people has arrived at in endeavoring to make the survival task easier. Often there is actually an involved technology associated with gathering food, making clothes, providing shelter, and so on. That is, there is a systematic and concerted effort associated with gathering and transmitting the knowledge of how these things can be done. Recipes for action can and often do become very sophisticated in today's world. The fact that one group of people has mechanized agriculture and supports agricultural research while another simply gathers food represents an obvious but critical difference between their cultural worlds. It represents a difference in their way of doing as well as a difference in their way of thinking about doing and of thinking about life in general. We could hardly talk about the sociocultural influences on behavior and development in the 20th century without mentioning TV, computers, and antibiotics; neither could we ignore supersonic jets, autos, and industrial pollution. Such products not only change ways of doing things—that is, provide us with new techniques, styles, and means—but they also drastically alter the world, or the environment, in which these things are done.

Consider yet another example from a slightly different sphere of life. Young mothers throughout the world experience some of the same basic problems with their children—what to feed them, how to clothe them, how and when to train them, and whether and how to teach them. You don't have to read Margaret Mead, however, to know that mothers' solutions to these problems vary. But what is important to us here is that it probably is not altogether the mother's solution in any case. It is a solution that is prominent within her social group and that has been transmitted to her through a medium to which she is particularly sensitive. My wife derived her child-rearing style partly from experienced elders (such as her neighbor) but mostly from recognized authorities (such as Dr. Spock). There were available solutions for her, as there are for mothers across the world. What those solutions are—that is, what style of child rearing is favored— is also part and parcel of that complex of guidelines called culture.

Summary. In brief, it may be said that each cultural group is characterized by guidelines for perceiving, explaining, judging, and doing. But although the same basic normative questions may be asked, groups differ because the answers to these questions will not be the same. When we use the term "culture," we are primarily referring to the complex of such guidelines that exists for any interdependent group of people.

CLASS

In discussing the sociocultural origins of behavior, the term "social class" is often used interchangeably with the term "culture." Indeed, there is probably some overlap in the two terms. When we refer to a child from the "middle class," there is some implicit reference to a style of life or cultural background. However, the concept of social class suggests dimensions of the social world that are not clearly designated by the term "culture." It therefore deserves treatment in its own right.

STATUS AND POWER

The term "social class" might best be reserved for referring to the way in which a society is stratified according to status and power. Any group of people is more than rules and roles, styles and preferences. Even within the smallest and most ephemeral of groups, a status system of some kind is bound to emerge. On university faculties there are professorial ranks and special chairs—for example, full, associate, and assistant professors, lecturers, "TAs," the Harley Jones Professor of Social Science, and so on. In my son's third-grade class, one or two children are invariably chosen as leaders and receive popular attention and group admiration; a group generally held in lower esteem and many other children falling somewhere between the two extremes complete the status ranking. Although I haven't really checked this out, I strongly suspect that there are the beginnings of such hierarchies in my daughter's preschool group, for such status differentiation begins at an early age. And of course, when you consider broader collectivities of persons, such as a community, there seem to be those who have higher or lower status.

Stratification of members into a status hierarchy of some kind is typical of group behavior. Social class, then, refers to a designated level of status within a given society. In feudal Europe there were three major classes or strata of society: the First Estate, consisting of the higher clergy; the Second Estate, consisting of secular noblemen; and the Third Estate, which comprised everyone else. In studies of contemporary American society, it is common to refer to some socioeconomic divisions, such as upper class, middle class, working class, and lower class.

The *way* in which status is attributed varies from society to society.

Individuals in some groups are accorded status by virtue of birth, without any real achievement on their part—that is, status is *ascribed* to them. The Queen of England and the tribal leader in Africa, for example, are what they are by virtue of birth. Status and power have been ascribed to them because of the order of their birth into certain families.

In other cases, *achievement* is at the basis of status. The status accorded a Nobel Prize winner is based on what he has accomplished. Of course, when status is accorded in this way, different types of achievement will have greater weight. Thus, within the United States, economic success seems to win a measure of status. At various times and places, heroism in war also has created at least a moment of glory for individuals; sometimes it was sufficient to ensure continuing status. However, as the veteran of Vietnam knows, war is not necessarily the way to fame and fortune. More often than not, the veteran is confronted with hostility rather than with glory upon his return. In certain adolescent societies, athletic prowess assures status, but scholarship does not (see Coleman, 1961).

When a group ascribes status on the basis of achievement, there tends to be greater movement in the status system. Thus, within highly industrialized societies, which depend heavily on technical competence and achievement, we can reasonably expect individual achievement to take precedence over birth, opening up possibilities for rapid status changes. When a tribal or agrarian society suddenly becomes industrialized, the status system based on ascription receives a serious jolt. Industry needs achievers and accords them status, or at least the accouterments of status, regardless of birth and family ties.

CLASS AND THE PERSON

Stratification appreciably affects the individual's social world. Persons at the upper level of any status hierarchy typically command a disproportionate share of the group's resources. They exert greater influences on others and, in general, have greater access to the institutions, services, and opportunities available within a group. Although high status is not necessarily good as far as any specific individual is concerned (Durkheim, 1958), low status usually has negative effects. The ghetto child soon learns that he exists at a different point on the status hierarchy than the suburban child does. It is impossible for him to command the same resources, and he does not have access to the same groups, activities, and experiences. Moreover, others may judge, respond, and relate to him in terms of his class membership rather than in terms of who he is. Thus, birth origins may affect the child's self-esteem as well as his behavior (Proshansky & Newton,

1968). This aspect of status should be important to the teacher or to anyone attempting to help individuals actualize their potential.

Individuals at any level of the status hierarchy typically are physically and socially isolated from people at other levels. As a result, a different way of life or a different cultural pattern is likely to emerge. The lower-class child, for example, will typically live in a neighborhood with other lower-class children. These children will have a pattern of experience that is different from the experience pattern of children in the upper classes. It is not surprising that they will exhibit styles and standards that differ from those of suburban children. Class is not equivalent to culture, but insofar as it designates a pattern of interpersonal communication and interaction and specifies opportunities for experience, it does tend to be associated with the development of distinct cultural patterns.

REFERENCE GROUPS

A basic assumption thus far has been that certain groups are significant to each individual. Culture is a complex of normative guidelines and styles that impinges on an individual as a member of a certain group. Class, too, refers to a group of people that, in some sense, has an influence on the person. In choosing, thinking, talking, and simply being human, a person refers to and acts in terms of groups that are significant to him. A society as a whole often is an important reference group. When traveling outside their country, Americans feel consciously American. Social class and socioeconomic or vocational groups also provide frameworks for action. Regardless of my perception of independence, my life is ordered by my role as "professor." (My wife contends that I do not even communicate well with nonprofessorial relatives—but then, who does communicate well with relatives?) My professional colleagues and I are not unique; everyone is in some sense isolated within role and class categories. Either by circumstance or by choice, an individual also responds to smaller segments of a larger society or class. Each of us has various specialized and limited reference groups that conform in some way to general standards and guidelines of the society or class in which we hold membership. Thus, the culture that is said to exist for a large group of persons always is translated in idiosyncratic ways by smaller, more specific groups. What these small groups are and how they function are critical in the determination of the sociocultural origins of achievement.

The family is a first and pervasively important reference group. Regardless of culture, human beings are unconditionally dependent upon others at birth. Almost invariably, some type of family unit exists to meet the needs of an infant and, in the course of doing so, becomes the primary group for transmitting the norms that will be the culture for that person. Families vary in terms of the culture they present, and, in considering the sociocultural origins of an individual's behavior, we cannot ignore the culture transmitted within this primary socialization unit. Perhaps in our attempts to better the lot of impoverished groups, we ought to be more concerned with the family than with the school. It has been repeatedly pointed out that the family life of the urban poor, although it often exemplifies a creative adaptation to oppression and dire need, does not facilitate adaptation to school, to job, or to other segments of the wider culture (Rainwater, 1966). It may well be that significant learning must begin and continue in the home if the child is to actualize his potential in any area of achievement.

But the family is not the only group to which the individual refers in making his choices, developing his beliefs, and adapting his behavior. Early in the course of development, children establish relationships with other groups that may become important to them. The norms of these groups may or may not agree with the norms extant in the family. Thus, it is very common for play and peer groups to emerge in childhood and to become increasingly important in framing the child's behavior. In all cultures, peer groups play important roles. In *Coming of Age in Samoa,* Margaret Mead (1928) showed how sex education in this more or less exotic culture was conveniently, and apparently successfully, handled by older peers. Despite the millions of dollars spent on the development of formal sex education in U. S. schools, the peer group is still responsible for inculcating knowledge about sex or at least for establishing behavioral norms. Similarly, parents lecture about justice and altruism, but there is some reason to believe that peer groups establish the norms in these areas.

We typically become interested in peer groups when they espouse behavior different from that espoused by another reference group such as the family. This occurs frequently, particularly in societies such as our own. Bronfenbrenner (1970), for example, has pointed out that parents in the United States tend to have less interaction with their children than do parents in other countries such as the U. S. S. R. Because children are isolated from adults, peer groups have greater significance for children and are more likely to present discrepant cultural frameworks. The "generation gap" shows that the family is not the only reference group of significance. Peer reference groups can be as critical in determining behavior and achievement as the family, the school, or even the child's "aptitude." Parents and teachers may hope for scholarship, but a peer group that values athletic accomplishment to the exclusion of scholarship wins out for many a high schooler (see Coleman, 1961).

Face-to-face reference groups are not the only significant ones. More remote groups are often important and may be remote only in a physical sense. For example, the life and behavior of a physician are to some degree determined by other physicians, most of whom he has never seen. Similarly, school superintendents look to other school superintendents (perhaps known only in their writings) for solutions to problems and for advice on playing their role. Individuals refer to those in the same social position or vocational category for guidelines for action. Professional organizations, labor unions, and church groups set styles of behavior without the necessity of face-to-face interaction. Mass media have led to a great increase in the number and the influence of such remote or secondary reference groups.

THE PERSONAL EXPERIENCE OF CULTURE

The discussion of reference groups makes it clear that many groups impinge on the individual. We can observe commonalities in behavioral guidelines that exist for any designated group. These commonalities we call a "culture." However, these guidelines are always translated for and transmitted to individuals by smaller groups that vary in the degree to which they share in that culture. Simply because we are brought up by different persons, each of us apprehends a different culture—only slightly different, perhaps, but different nevertheless. The existence of various reference groups with which a person may choose to identify further shows that the sociocultural world of an individual is a very personal and subjective thing. We can identify groups that share similar answers to basic normative questions. We can describe opportunities, alternatives, experiences, and styles that are objectively present in a given context. But finally, the sociocultural world that exists for you, me, or anyone else is a highly particularized and subjective one. The objective analysis of culture and social environment is a desirable and necessary first step in understanding the behavior of children. It should, however, not be the last step in understanding a child.

CHAPTER
THREE
CULTURE AND THE
CAPACITY
TO ACHIEVE

That children of differing sociocultural origins also differ in patterns of achievement is nearly undeniable. We did not need the Coleman Report to discover that fact. Any teacher experienced in teaching children from culturally diverse groups has discovered it many times over. In attempting to clarify and explain these differing patterns in achievement, teachers as well as researchers have found it convenient to refer to two major categories of immediate cause: "intellectual capacity" and "motivation." Such a distinction between reason and will is probably comfortable for most of us, products of a Western heritage as we are. Without claiming that the distinction is valid—only that it is convenient—I will use it. Chapters Four and Five deal with the motivation to achieve, while this chapter is concerned with the intellectual capacity to achieve.

INTELLECTUAL CAPACITY

It is probably true that some sort of intellectual readiness is basic to achievement in most areas. Certainly, when one considers the kind of accomplishments that schools (in almost any cultural context) value and promote, there can be little doubt that the acquisition and utilization of knowledge of some kind are involved. As a matter of fact, the whole business of school seems, in one sense or another, to be tied up with cognitive growth. Indeed, whether one talks about achievement in school, athletics, industry, or politics, the intellectual component can hardly be ignored. This is all by way of suggesting that, in considering achievement, it is important to consider the nature of intellect. And, of course, within the context of this book, the overriding question is whether or how sociocultural factors affect intellect.

Although it is easy enough to assert that "intellectual capacity" is in some sense crucial to achievement, it is not at all easy to define "intellectual capacity." Generally, it refers to a presumed potential for solving problems, engaging in abstract reasoning, and benefiting from experience.

Certain people just seem to be more prepared to do these things than others. Some 6-year-olds read on the first day of school; others never acquire this skill. Similarly, some adults readily design computers; others are unable to punch a data card correctly. Such variation in performance serves as a basis for the inference that people differ in intellectual capacity.

However we wish to define this capacity, there are at least three facets to it that have special relevance—especially when we consider the problems of teaching children of diverse sociocultural backgrounds. These three facets of intellectual capacity are language, perception, and cognition.

CULTURE AND LANGUAGE

When we consider the reasons why disadvantaged children do not achieve, language emerges as a factor of major importance. When a child grows up as a member of an ethnic minority, his first language probably is not the language spoken and used in school. This is not only true of the manifestly bilingual Chicano child but also true of the black or Appalachian child who speaks English—though not a standard version. It is not that his cultural background has deprived him of an effective language. It *has* given him a useful and in many ways a very colorful and interesting language—so interesting and colorful in fact that the language of the "impoverished minority" often finds its way into "standard English." Thus, words and concepts such as *rapping* and *jiving* are just too good not to be given rather general and wide usage. However, the language that a member of an impoverished minority receives as part of his cultural background is *not* the language that he is expected to employ in school—and therein lies a major problem.

Such a language discrepancy is likely to affect the minority-group child's perception of school and his interaction with teachers. Having the "wrong" language certainly will not make him feel at home in the school. It is likely to cause him to view school and teachers as objects from another world and, therefore, as strange or even hostile. This will affect the child's motivation to perform and will certainly inhibit his understanding of what is expected of him. While this may be obvious to some, the sad fact is that teachers are often unaware of the profound importance of the problem. They do not always recognize that, in addition to an accent, the black, Chicano, or Puerto Rican child, in a very real sense has his own language. Even when bilingualism is recognized, as in the case of children from Spanish-speaking families, there is still a perceptible tendency to denigrate one language (and associated culture?) in order to impose another (Gumperz & Hernández-Chavez, 1972).

That the teacher uses one language and the child another obviously is a problem as far as social interaction is concerned. It is also a problem as far as teaching is concerned, but it is not just a matter of teacher and pupil using different words or grammar. It is, more importantly, that, in the use of such different words and grammar, teacher and student are in effect apprehending different worlds. A number of years ago, Benjamin Lee Whorf (1956) proposed what has come to be known as the linguistic-relativity hypothesis. The basic and substantive point of this hypothesis is that somehow our language determines how we think and, in general, how we perceive and comprehend the world. Thus, as the child learns a language, he learns to see and to think as well as to speak.[1]

Carried to its extreme, this hypothesis probably is not tenable. Yet, several things seem quite clear in this regard. A person does tend to categorize his world in terms of the concepts provided by the language he uses (Cole, 1972). To use an example suggested by Brown (1965), the Hanunóo, a Filipino tribal group, have names for 92 varieties of rice. To the typical American, rice is rice is rice. This differential category system seems to have two important correlates. First, the typical American would probably have difficulty recognizing and distinguishing more than a few kinds of rice. Second, if he did recognize certain differences, he may well have difficulty remembering them, for it seems that, in order to retain any experience in memory, it is important that it be effectively translated into one's particular category system. The point, of course, is that, as the child learns a group's language, he also absorbs the thought pattern of the group. He learns what is important among objects and things. He is provided with a perceptual selection system and a way of categorizing his thoughts.

Now consider once again our teacher and student from different cultural origins. It is not only that their words are mutually strange, and social interaction is therefore affected. In a very real sense, they are perceiving, conceptualizing, and talking about different worlds. The teacher, perhaps largely in an unconscious way, assumes that the child possesses the same conceptual system that he or she does, even though the child obviously uses a different grammar and some strange words. The teacher then attempts to build on and to teach with reference to such a *presumed* shared conceptual system. No wonder the student responds with a blank face or limited achievement. Even more than that, the child simply cannot translate many of the classroom experiences into his own language. As a result, it is difficult if not impossible for him to retain these experiences for future use.

A major problem confronting the minority-group child is that he possesses the "wrong" language or that he must cope with multiple languages (see Gumperz & Hernández-Chavez, 1972). But is it also possible

---

[1] For a critical review of the literature related to this hypothesis, see Miller and McNeill (1968).

that he does not have enough skill at his own language to succeed in a school situation? This is still a question of some debate, but it is an issue that cannot be avoided.

On the one hand, students (such as Labov, 1970) of the language and dialects of various impoverished social groups have emphasized that these languages are fully sufficient—that is, they can convey whatever thought is necessary or desired. The so-called disadvantaged child has not been deprived of a vocabulary. Rather, he has simply acquired one in accord with the "vocabulary pool" of his speech community. Thus, those who judge this child to be lacking in linguistic competence do so because they measure the child in terms of a speech community with which the child has had little interaction. Naturally, the child does not typically use or have knowledge of words that are not common in his speech community. This does not mean, however, that he possesses a meager vocabulary. It is further argued that what is often judged to be a deficiency in grammar is only a difference. In itself, the difference does not inhibit problem solving, learning, or the acquisition of skills. It simply impedes communication with those who know and accept only another style (Shuy, 1969; Goodman, 1969). Those who hold this view maintain that minority-group children do not fail in school because of a language deficiency; instead, they fail because teachers don't allow them to utilize the potential of their first language—be it Spanish, Cherokee, or a black dialect—as a means of acquiring basic skills and as an instrument to learning the necessary second language, standard English (Baratz & Baratz, 1970; John, 1972). A major implication of this, of course, is that early-childhood programs or other programs that are specifically geared to deal with language *deprivation* (see, for example, Bereiter & Engelmann, 1966; Bereiter, 1968; Engelmann, 1970) are both prejudicial and counterproductive.

While not directly questioning the worth or sufficiency of the language available or in use within a particular impoverished community, we still may question whether the typical disadvantaged child has truly developed the linguistic competence necessary for effective school performance. It is difficult to deny that the language training experienced by the child varies drastically with socioeconomic level (see Bernstein, 1970; Hunt, 1971, 1972, in preparation; Hunt & Kirk, 1971; Jensen, 1968). Studies show that parents of lower *socioeconomic status* (SES) spend less time in verbal interaction with their children (Milner, 1951) and also differ from upper-SES parents in the way in which they interact verbally with their children.[2] While the impoverished child may get one-word replies,

---

[2] We might logically wonder about the role of siblings and peers in verbal training. To what extent, for example, can they supplement or enhance parental training? Unfortunately, there are no definitive studies at this point.

children from the upper classes receive explanations. Children from the upper classes are characteristically taught how to use language, and they regularly experience the power of language in providing guidelines for solving problems (Hess & Shipman, 1967). Developmental psychologists such as Hunt (1969) find it difficult to ignore these differences and tend to suppose that the typical disadvantaged child is somewhat deficient in language skills. Consequently, they contend that any attempt to deal with the problem must begin with the home. Changing school practices alone will not do the job. Basic language patterns important in school achievement must be set in early childhood. In order to ensure that these patterns are set, parents must be trained to be effective teachers of language and its associated processes.

The argument over the nature of the language problem may not be so pointed as I have made it seem. Some have focused on the structure of language spoken by a community and have found that it is adequate. Therefore, they have encouraged educators to accept the child's linguistic patterns, to build upon them, and to test in terms of them. Others, who focus on differential child-rearing practices, have questioned the sufficiency of the typical disadvantaged child's language skills. These psychologists may advocate remedial language training as a solution, but, more appropriately, they recommend working on parental child-rearing practices. This may seem like a serious and irresolvable argument, but, actually, both perspectives are probably necessary in attempting to deal effectively with the situation. At any rate, the evidence does not clearly and unequivocably support either perspective.

CULTURE AND PERCEPTION

People from different cultures not only speak different languages but also perceive different worlds. Given the same array of objects, things, and events, different items and configurations will be selected and ignored and different combinations of things and events will be related or dissociated. In a very real sense, cultural origin shapes or determines the world we think and talk about as well as the world we see, hear, touch, and smell. It is relatively easy to demonstrate that individuals from different cultures select and differentiate in contrasting manners. Doubtless, language is one medium for prompting or reinforcing such tendencies. Certain Eskimo groups have words for and clearly recognize three or more different kinds of snow. It's a good guess that their discrimination among types of snow is better than that of the Aztec, whose language employs one word for those phenomena that most of us refer to separately as *cold, ice,* and *snow* (Whorf, 1940, 1956). Similarly, the Arabs have 6,000 words for camel, and they presumably recognize a special kind of beast commensurate to each category (Thomas, 1937). To me and to those whom I know, there can't be more than two kinds of camels: one-humped and two-humped. But in defense of me and my friends, I would immediately add that we are better than most camel herders in distinguishing automobiles. Somehow differential cultural experiences have focused our perceptions in one way or another.

Considerable cross-cultural research has indicated that, in addition to affecting what we select to see or the facility with which we can differentiate, cultural experiences also affect the manner in which we organize our sensations. Individuals who grow up in a Western and "well-carpentered"[3] world are subject to certain perceptual illusions. Let's consider one.

Figure 3.1 presents a schematic drawing of the rod-and-frame illusion that has entertained and sometimes educated many an introductory psychology class. You may recall that, when the frame rotates on a black velvet background, it is seen as an oscillating *rectangular* window frame. However, it is really *trapezoidal,* and it is rotating, not oscillating. But since a rectangular window frame usually impinges itself on our eyes as a trapezoid, it is natural to assume that this is just another case of an actually rectangular window that just happens to look trapezoidal from our angle. After all, whoever heard of a trapezoidal window frame? So that particular perception will make sense, an illusion of oscillation is created. Of course, none of us who have viewed this contraption has ever thought the matter out in just this way. It has all happened quite automatically. We have simply constructed and organized events in a way that makes sense within our experience. The task is commonplace, and that's why it is done with nary a thought, automatically—that is, automatically in our culture. It appears, however, that in a less-carpentered culture—a culture in which windows are not commonplace and rectangularity is not part and parcel of everyone's life—the illusion is not automatic. Allport and Pettigrew (1957), for example, found that rural Zulus in Africa were less likely to see a rectangle oscillating than were urban Zulus. Both groups were less predisposed to the rectangle illusion than were Europeans.

Other examples illustrate that the experiences determined by a culture can, to a significant degree, affect the world that is seen. A person's sociocultural origins predispose him to attend to some items and ignore others. The experiences that may be available to this or that group will

[3] Segall, Campbell, and Herskovitz (1966) are responsible for characterizing environments as "carpentered." This expression refers specifically to the tendency of objects in the environment to be characterized by rectangles, straight lines, and right angles. Western environments most often typify such "carpenteredness."

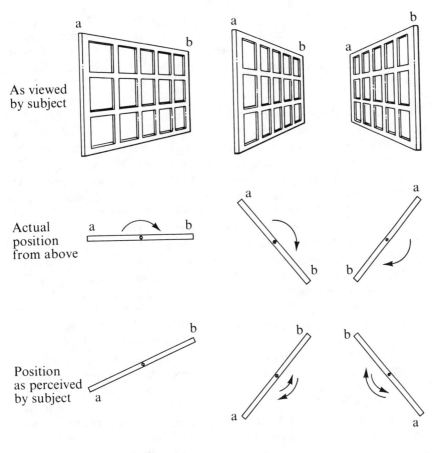

As viewed
by subject

Actual
position
from above

Position
as perceived
by subject

Position 1   Position 2   Position 3

Figure 3.1. Illusion created by rotating a trapezoidal window. The window is so constructed that in Position 1 it looks like a rectangular window with the left edge closer to the subject. Actually the left edge (*a*) and the right edge (*b*) are equally distant from the observer. As the window rotates clockwise (as viewed from above), the left edge remains larger to the subject than the right edge; hence, it still seems nearer, even though it is moving away (Position 2). Even when the window rotates completely—goes through what would be twelve o'clock on a clock and begins to come closer again (Position 3)—*a* is still seen as closer than *b*. The viewer then tends to see the window as waving back and forth rather than as going around. From Hilgard, E. R., and Atkinson, R. C. *Introduction to Psychology,* 4th ed., Harcourt Brace Jovanovich, 1967; adapted from A. Ames, Visual perception and the rotating trapezoidal window. *Psychological Monographs,* 1951, **65**(324). Copyright 1951 by the American Psychological Association. Reprinted by permission of Harcourt Brace Jovanovich and the American Psychological Association.

provide different perceptual predispositions and ways of interpreting sensory input. The role of learning and experience in affecting perception is an important facet of human development. There are also instances in which this issue can become a very practical and relevant matter to the teacher.

It is typically assumed that pictures are effective teaching devices. Presumably, children lacking in language, previous learning experiences, or inclination toward abstractions can still apprehend the message of a picture. After all, using a picture to say, show, or explain something is just like using the real thing. Or is it? Seldom do we stop to think that the effective use of pictures may, in fact, depend on prior learning experiences. Yet, a series of studies conducted in South Africa (Hudson, 1960, 1962; Mundy-Castle & Nelson, 1962; Mundy-Castle, 1966), Sierra Leone (Dawson, 1963), and the West Indies and England (Vernon, 1965) seems to indicate just that. When children have little or no experience with the language of event simulation that is employed in pictures, they are prone to misconstrue the pictorial cues and gain little benefit from this presumed teaching aid. The typical 10-year-old who has been exposed to picture books, TV, and movies would describe the pictures in Figure 3.2 in such a way that it would be obvious that the hunter is focusing on the antelope rather than on the elephant, which is in the background and at a distance. This response clearly takes certain depth cues into account. But the Ghanaian child without such experience is likely to misinterpret these pictures completely. Mundy-Castle (1966) found that such children were likely to report that the spear was aimed at the elephant rather than at the antelope in cards 1 through 4 and that, in card 1, the man was unable to even see the antelope because the hill was blocking his vision. The Ghanaian children were apparently not employing the depth cues that the Westerner so readily employs. These studies also show that, after they attend school, African children begin using depth cues. This finding reinforces the belief that their "deficit" in pictorial depth perception is a result of early experiences established by the children's sociocultural origins. We cannot help but wonder how typical visual aids will work out in cultures such as those studied by Mundy-Castle. It is perhaps true that a picture is worth a thousand words. But what kind of picture? What kind of worth? And for what culture? Pictures are not a universal language. How we represent things pictorially is as much a part of our cultural heritage as the clothes we wear—though perhaps more subtly so (see Cole, 1972).

Social experiences do, indeed, affect perception. Moreover, they can affect it in ways that may be crucial as far as the acquisition of knowledge and achievement in general are concerned. That is made quite clear by research in cultures drastically different from our own. Such research stimulates an important question: is it possible that such socially deter-

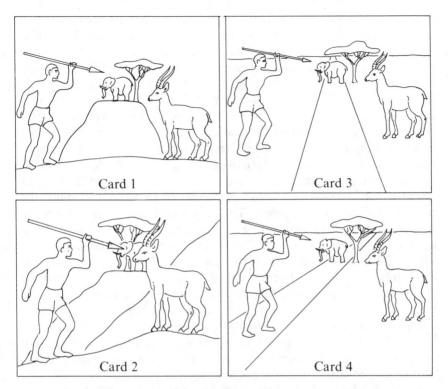

Figure 3.2. Pictures used by Mundy-Castle. From Mundy-Castle, A. C. Pictorial depth in Ghanaian children. *International Journal of Psychology,* 1966, **1**, 290–300, by permission of the International Union of Psychological Science and Dunod Editeur, Paris.

mined predispositions also play a significant role in the differential achievement among culturally diverse groups within the United States?

Perhaps the poor child in the inner city of Chicago, every bit as much as the Ghanaian child, has early perceptual experiences that are critically different from those of the child raised in the "typical" home. Perhaps these experiences do significantly inhibit his behavior in the classroom. We would be surprised if the Ghanaian children described earlier had no difficulty in adjusting to schooling experiences dependent on pictorial representation. Perhaps the differences in perceptual predisposition of students within our own national borders are more subtle, yet they are equally real and equally important.

A final answer to this line of questioning cannot as yet be given. However, current research indicates that perceptual experience, particularly in the early years, does vary among socioeconomic and cultural groups within the United States. It also appears that this variation has some important effects as far as achievement in the standard American school is concerned. The poor child is likely to come from a home environment that does not facilitate perceptual discrimination (Deutsch, 1964; Deutsch & Brown, 1964). At least superficially, the home of the poor child seems poorly designed for any type of focused perceptual training. It is crowded and cluttered, it lacks toys and objects that guide perceptual learning, and it is characterized by the kind of overwhelming sensory experience that is likely to be counterproductive. Certainly, the perceptual experiences available in the home of the poor child do not seem to be especially beneficial or preparatory to schooling. The home is devoid of pictures and books, and, most importantly, it is lacking in adults who can or do devote effort to assisting the child in learning to "read pictures," label discriminations, and attend to relationships. In terms of preparation for standard schooling, the poor child seems to be deprived. That is, he apparently does not possess the discrimination, categorizing, and attending skills that schoolchildren are expected to have (Deutsch, 1968). Interestingly enough, research by Sigel (1970) also indicates that the poor child is not unlike Ghanaian children in his inability to interact with pictures as replacements for objects. It is difficult not to suppose that these extraschool perceptual experiences have had their effects and are in some sense at the base of the difficulties in achievement that have been amply documented.

These apparent differences in early perceptual experiences may also have pervasive and persistent effects on the child's readiness to learn. That is, his intellectual development is likely to be profoundly affected. The research of White (1967; White & Held, 1966; White, Castle, & Held, 1964) and Hunt (1972) makes this hypothesis especially persuasive. Collectively, their research has indicated that a limited sensory experience in the early years is likely to inhibit intellectual development. Thus, children in orphanages or foundling homes, who lie in cribs on white sheets without the benefit of colorful mobiles and stabiles, show a retarded development, at least in regard to the early-appearing sensory and motor competencies. However, the development of these children can be increased by providing appropriate sensory experiences. As a matter of fact, White was able to accelerate the development of infants in a New Jersey institution to a degree that was not attained by the offspring of young faculty members and graduate students studied by Hunt (1969, p. 134). Sensorimotor development seems to be an important early stage in cognitive development.

CULTURE AND COGNITION

Language and perceptual predispositions are basic to the capacity to achieve; yet, we cannot conveniently fit all that is important in this regard under these two rubrics. We have thus far virtually ignored such matters as the development of patterns of processing information and of solving problems. It is to these matters that we now turn.

Throughout the years, world travelers, anthropologists, and, more recently, psychologists have noticed some interesting differences in the thought processes of Western Europeans and primitives—differences that could not be readily attributed to language, perceptual bias, or belief systems. There just seemed to be many instances in which primitives processed information, reflected on it, and solved problems with it in ways quite different from Europeans.

Thus, for example, it has been repeatedly noted that primitives in Africa possess a remarkable ability to remember certain things and events but a seeming inability to learn and remember in the more structured fashion required in school. Bartlett (1932) relates that a Swazi cowherd was able to repeat in the most intricate detail the features of a business transaction that had occurred at least a year in the past. The cowherd had been only peripherally involved in the transaction but nevertheless was able to recall identifying marks of the cattle and the price paid in each instance with only a few errors. And this is but one of many examples of the capacity to accurately recall a considerable amount of information. Yet when it comes to learning lists of items dissociated from an event context, this cowherd and his colleagues often seem woefully inadequate. There may be an interest or motivational factor involved here. Cowherds find it in their interest to remember a great deal about cows. My sons amaze me with their recall of names and statistics associated with any sport that receives an airing on TV. More than interest may be involved, however. Michael Cole (1972) has suggested that some type of culturally based "learning to learn" is also importantly involved. The primitive develops an approach to learning and memory that is based on the structure and characteristics implicit within a concrete event. In contrast, the European develops an approach to learning based on an imposed, abstract structure. Thus, when a European schoolboy is presented with a series of items to commit to memory, he will tend to group these according to semantic categories and later reproduce them in terms of these categories. The African schoolboy soon learns to "cluster" in this way also. The unschooled primitive, however, has difficulty in such free recall unless the items are tied to concrete events. Moreover, it seems that the more "natural" way for the primitive to recall items is in terms of the flow of events as they occur—for example, in a narrative. Apparently, there is little reason to believe that the primitive has a poor memory. These *is* reason to believe that his style of apprehending, retaining, and recalling items is different. Western culture and Western schools are associated with memory strategies that impose abstract and primarily semantic categories on events to be remembered. Many a Western preschooler absorbs this style before entering school. If not, it is likely that he will learn it in the course of schooling—with plenty of help from home. According to Cole, the typical unschooled primitive does not acquire this style, and, thus, in Western-style tests of memory, he performs poorly. It is not that he cannot learn or that his memory is deficient. Rather, he has not learned to learn according to the rules of another culture.

There are other examples of how learning strategies can be affected by early cultural experience. Collectively, all of them suggest that, within each cultural context, early experience is provided in how to learn. It is only a short step to conclude that the readiness to achieve in school is significantly dependent on the learning strategies acquired by the child and on the strategies required by the curriculum. There are, of course, many facets to this issue that could be pursued further—not the least of which is the possibility that learning "deficits" of minority-group children are in fact differences in acquired learning strategies rather than deficits in intellectual development (Cole & Bruner, 1971). However, prolonging discussion on this point might prevent us from raising a very basic question about the nature of cognitive development. That basic question relates to the development of logic. It is often implied and sometimes suggested directly that cultures that are closely tied to direct and concrete experiences may well inhibit the development of abstract thinking in the child. His cognitive development may be arrested at a stage that prevents him from engaging in the kinds of behavior that we associate with science making, for example. That is a serious and disturbing assertion, for it implies that the nature of science and the teaching of science will necessarily vary from culture to culture.

To a considerable extent, the discussion on this point has revolved around the work of Jean Piaget, his students, and his followers.[4] Piaget has been concerned primarily with the question of what is essentially human about human thought. That is to say, he is concerned with how the human species in general acquires knowledge instead of with how people become enculturated or acquire skills and thought patterns as a function of group membership. In the course of studying children in Geneva, Switzerland, he has formulated principles regarding the unfolding of thought that may well characterize humans generally. According to Piaget, the child-person goes through four sequential stages of cognitive development: (1) sensorimotor, (2) preoperational thought, (3) concrete operations, and (4) formal operations.

The first or *sensorimotor stage* is believed to span approximately

[4] Piaget's writings are extensive, and it is therefore helpful to refer the interested student to introductory but thorough reviews such as those by Flavell (1963), Phillips (1969), and Ginsburg and Opper (1969).

the first 18 months of life. The major "task" of the child during this period
is to achieve some kind of perceptual regularity in his world. This stage is
assumed to end when the child seems to be capable of imagery or of
representing things to himself mentally. Consider for a moment the kinds
of problems that the infant must solve during this period. Earlier we saw
that early learning regarding the shapes of windows may, in unusual instances, cause us to make errors. Usually, however, such learning does not
mislead us. Indeed, it is a most critical thing, regardless of culture, to learn
that an object looked at from different perspectives is still the same object
even though its shape, size, and perhaps color may be continually changing
as far as actual stimulation on the visual receptors is concerned. As objects,
persons, and things move about in space, they leave physically different im-
pressions on our sensory organs. If our life is to have any order whatsoever,
we must somehow readily and automatically account for these differences.
As adults, we typically do this. When I look at the textbook on my desk,
I see a rectangular object. As I get up to stretch and light my pipe, that
book is still a rectangular object, and I still *see* the same book. I doubt
whether I could impress my 10-year-old son with that fact, but anyone
interested in human behavior ought to be profoundly impressed. The reason
is this: in order for that book to be perceived as constant and to have a
stable identity, my brain had to make an important contribution. It had to
reconstruct the situation according to certain abiding assumptions about
the shape of books, the experiencing of booklike things on desks, and what
or who was moving in this situation. The constant and stable book is as
much a product of me as it is a function of the light waves that happen to
strike the retina of my eyes.

Somehow the child invariably arrives at such ordered constructions
of the world. Clearly he must do this if he is to move about with minimal
distraction and with a measure of facility. When such imaging seems to be
present, the child is said to enter a second stage, referred to as the stage
of *preoperational* thought. It spans the years from 2 to 7 and is characterized by increased sophistication in handling the perceptual world. At the
same time, however, the child still tends to be dominated by his perceptions
and by the "actual situation" that confronts him. The child's mental functioning during this period can best be shown by a series of experiments.
First, consider a demonstration of what has come to be called conservation.
The term "conservation" refers to the knowledge that a primary property
of something, such as its volume, will remain the same regardless of its
particular shape. You and I know that a round chunk of clay does not
change in volume when we transform it into a snakelike shape. It is still
the same hunk of clay. The child in the preoperational-thought stage has
arrived at many basic constancies and identities, but he still has trouble

with this one. To demonstrate this for yourself, try this problem first with a 4-year-old and then with a 10-year-old. Pour an equal amount of milk, water, or Kool-aid into two glasses (A and B), as illustrated in Figure 3.3. Make sure the child agrees that there is the same amount of liquid in each glass. Then pour the liquid from one of the glasses into the beaker (C). Now ask the child whether B and C contain the same amount. The 4-year-old will typically say "no" and will maintain that C contains more. Even if you go back through the process, showing him that A and B are equal, he will continue to insist that C contains more. Of course, when you try this with a 10-year-old, he will not only give you the correct answer but also let you know that he considers this line of questioning ridiculous.

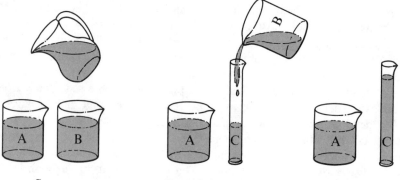

Same   Pour B into C   Still same?

Figure 3.3.   Illustration of the liquid conservation experiment. Equal amounts of liquid are poured into two glasses, and the child is asked to confirm that the glasses hold the same amount. Then the liquid from one of the glasses is poured into a tall, narrow beaker, and the child is asked to compare the amount of liquid in glass A with the amount in beaker C. Although older children readily grasp the fact that the change in the shape of the container does not change the amount of liquid, younger children will say that the beaker contains more liquid than the glass does—even when they have seen the liquid from the glass poured into the beaker.

Piaget suggests that such different responses of 4- and 10-year-olds are associated with important differences in intellectual functioning. To the 4-year-old, liquid in a beaker "looks" bigger. That is, he fixates on the dimension of height and is unable to alternately or simultaneously consider width. He is overwhelmed by the salience of one perceptual dimension and responds accordingly, without attempting to mentally correct for the fact that looks may be deceiving.

This absorption of the younger child with a salient and limited aspect of his perceptual world is part of a general tendency referred to as "egocentrism." In this case, egocentrism does not mean selfish pride or conceit. Rather, it refers to the child's inability to remove himself mentally from immediately experienced events and to assume another perspective. It is especially fascinating to consider how this inability operates in social behavior. When I ask my 3-year-old daughter how many brothers she has, she will quickly respond "two," proceed to name them ("Martin" and "Michael"), and smile with a satisfied smile of a job well done. When I ask her how many sisters she has, she will say "none" and again seemingly feel quite pleased with herself. If, however, I ask her how many brothers or sisters Martin (her oldest brother) has, she becomes confused and either proceeds to jabber away on another topic or makes a random, and almost always incorrect, guess. Perhaps she has learned certain relationships by rote. Piaget's theory suggests that something more is involved, and I am inclined to believe him. I suspect that, in this case, as in several others of which I am aware, she simply is unable to take the perspective of another.

After the age of 7, in the *concrete-operations stage,* the child will not make the conceptual errors that I've just described. The beaker experiment is no problem. He is now able to see things from the point of view of another. By this time, he is engaging in complex social behavior and creating his own groups, societies, and, if you will, culture. However, full conceptual development has not been reached.

The final stage, the *formal-operations stage,* occurs after the age of 12 and represents the final fruition of cognitive development. In this stage, the child begins to operate as a scientist. That is, he has the ability to solve the problems of his perceptual world, has effective modes of handling things and events that he directly experiences, and has the capacity to imagine possible, potential relationships among these objects. He can manipulate, change, reform, and transform them mentally and predict the result. That is, he can engage in the kind of hypothetical-deductive thinking that characterizes the scientist.

Let's consider an example of this type of reasoning. If Johnny, a 9-year-old student in your class, can't read, you might begin to work on his problem by constructing a theory regarding why he can't read. In constructing this theory, you probably would at least consider a number of different reasons that have been handed down to you by your teachers, by your colleagues, or by *Time* magazine. Good teachers would probably consider a variety of possibilities before actually making a judgment on Johnny and prescribing a course of action. That is, they might engage in some hypothetical experiments that would narrow down the range of possible causes of Johnny's problem. For example, if Johnny has recently come from Italy and can't speak English, that would be reason enough for his having difficulty in the typical American reading class. Eye weakness, a physical limitation, family discord, and general emotional instability are all factors to be considered. Mental experiments—analytically imagining the possible effect of one variable on another without actually manipulating or observing anything—might take the following form:

If X were the cause, then Y.

Y occurs. X must be the cause. Make plans to alleviate X. (Note that a hypothetical testing of plans would precede the actual choice of a plan.)

Y doesn't occur. X must not be the cause. Search elsewhere.

Thus, you run through a number of such mental experiments before you actually do something to test your thinking.

It is this hypothetical type of reasoning that is characteristic of the formal-operations stage. This kind of thought exemplifies the ultimate in intellectual transaction with the world. According to Piaget, such thinking comes into being during adolescence. Indeed, in most Western societies, we have come to expect this level of cognitive development from adolescents. It is during adolescence that the advantages and responsibilities of curricula are weighed and that mental experimentation in school, work, love, and courses of action is encouraged.

Especially when we consider Piaget's description of the last stage, it is impossible not to ask how general these stages are. Do all individuals, regardless of cultural experience, inevitably evolve toward an abstract and hypothetical-deductive mode of thought?

It is relatively easy to believe that certain experiences necessary to cognitive development will be present in every culture. The experiences and environmental demands associated with the development of object identity, for example, seem quite universal. Similarly, social living itself would almost demand the development of the ability to take different perspectives.

Those who have attempted to teach Western science in a non-Western culture, however, might wonder whether there is a universal tendency to develop toward a hypothetical-deductive mode of reasoning. The teacher of disadvantaged children might also wonder whether some social experiences prompt increased development in the abstract modes of thought of the latter Piagetian stages. The child in an African classroom seems so disinclined to hypothesize, experiment, or move from the given to the "might be" (see Brown, in preparation), and the so-called disadvantaged child in the United States seems so overwhelmingly predisposed to the concrete rather than to the abstract (Eisenberg, 1967).

The evidence, while by no means final, provides some interesting guidelines to our thinking here. Whether it is because the same basic experiences are virtually universal or because human nature is relatively invariant in this regard, the observed sequence of development described by Piaget holds fairly well across cultural groups (see Goodnow, 1962). There are, however, some important lines of evidence suggesting that the child's sociocultural origins may well modify his progression through the stages. Greenfield and Bruner (1969; Greenfield, 1966), for example, have reported evidence indicating that the school experience may be a major factor in accelerating this progression. Thus, in a study of conservation behavior among urban and rural, schooled and unschooled children of an African ethnocultural group (the Wolof), differences between the schooled and unschooled rural children were found to be greater than those between urban and rural children. Schoolchildren clearly achieved conservation at an earlier age than children who did not have this experience. The general conclusion that Bruner and Greenfield reached on the basis of this and other studies was that this acceleration of a more abstract mode of handling things is a natural and probably inevitable outcome of schooling. In primitive cultures, a person learns by imitation and through direct experience. As a matter of fact, teaching, as we know it, may not really be a major part of socialization in a primitive society. However, as a society develops in complexity, children are cut off from directly and immediately experiencing adults' behavior in response to critical life events. The primitive child participates in the hunt; the urban American child must be *told* how food gets to the table. The American child experiences adult behavior largely through the medium of language and in a context quite different from the one in which the actual events occur. Such an emphasis on "indirect experiencing" is really an emphasis on abstract thought. Thus, the whole idea of school is really associated with the development of abstract thought, and Bruner and Greenfield suggest that the institution of school, by itself, regardless of the specific curriculum, has a profound effect on cognitive growth. Perhaps school may be responsible for whether or not formal operations become modal in a culture. In any case, there is evidence that planned intervention can change something about cognition as Piaget describes it.

Bruner and Greenfield's research does seem to suggest that the cultural context can affect the development of logical thought. Following their evidence and associated reasoning, it does not seem likely that a scientific way of thinking will readily develop in a cultural context in which there is a lack of emphasis on treating events abstractly. Kohlberg (1969) has also reported evidence that, even when individuals exhibit an abstract mode of thinking, they may regress if the culture does not support such modes of logic. It may well be, then, that cultures and cultural contexts can deprive individuals of the modes of handling information that seem to be critical for advanced technological, scientific thinking and for general intellectual development. Before we accept this deprivation hypothesis, however, we should consider the possibility that the fact that abstract thinking is not used is a difference instead of a deprivation. Quite possibly, for example, Greenfield's Wolof children—with or without school—would exhibit abstract modes of reasoning if the appropriate context or setting were to be found. It is difficult not to believe that the standard Piagetian interview—regardless of whether it is conducted in the native language or with culturally familiar items—is not in some sense culturally biased. Aside from the problems in conducting such interviews with individuals who do not share the interviewer's culture (Kamara & Easley, in preparation), there is also the fact that the eliciting of behavior is still on the researcher's terms. Conceivably, there are settings, situations, and contexts in which the most scientific of thinking will be exhibited by the most primitive of primitives.

A PROBLEMATIC POSTSCRIPT

There is a study that has always especially fascinated me when I have thought about social experience and the capacity to achieve. That study, conducted by Gerald Lesser and his colleagues (Lesser, Fifer, & Clark, 1967; Stodolsky & Lesser, 1967), clearly lays before us the kinds of observed differences in capacity that intrigue the scholar but often plague the teacher. Lesser studied four different mental abilities (verbal, reasoning, number facility, and space conceptualization) among first-grade children from four different ethnic groups (Chinese, Jews, blacks, and Puerto Ricans) in New York City. Within each ethnic-group category, there were children from both lower and middle classes. As one might expect, the social-class level of the children was significantly related to their level of performance. Thus, middle-class children scored higher than lower-class subjects on all four tests. What was intriguing about the results was the pattern of variation in the abilities for each ethnic group. On verbal ability, for instance, Jewish children scored highest, blacks second, Chinese third, and Puerto Ricans fourth. However, on reasoning, the Chinese ranked first, the Jewish children second, blacks third, and Puerto Ricans last. In other words, what Lesser and his associates seemed to find was evidence that, within ethnic groups, there is a pattern of competence with regard to different areas of mental functioning.

In viewing these results, or any other results of this nature, there are several explanatory hypotheses that are usually suggested. Thus far,

I have repeatedly emphasized the role of experience in creating such differences. That is, I have focused the discussion on cultural deprivation and/or cultural differences that may explain differential performance. Certainly, in considering the Lesser results, it seems reasonable to relate a goodly share of this variation in pattern to the culturally provided opportunities to learn. Quite possibly, there are different experiences available to Chinese children that make them better at arithmetic—although we haven't identified these experiences as yet. Quite possibly, there is also something that Jewish families transfer to their children that increases their verbal competence. The Lesser results also indicate a consistent difference in level of performance associated with SES level across ethnic groups. This, too, might be explained largely by social-experience factors—a bias implicit in much of the preceding discussion. But the fact remains that, within a number of quarters, there is an unwillingness to accept the social-experience explanation as being totally valid. The most notable example here is found in the work of Arthur Jensen (1969).

Jensen has maintained that genetic or hereditary factors must be viewed as significant determinants, particularly in the case of black, disadvantaged children. Thus, it has been argued that, through a "selective-breeding" process, certain competencies have become prominent among the blacks who live in the United States, but that these competencies are not the same ones found more commonly in white children. One of these competencies that seems more typical for whites than for blacks is the ability to handle abstract reasoning. It just so happens that, at this point in time and in U. S. society, the capacity for abstract reasoning is highly valued, and therefore status is accorded to it. Other psychologists have used very similar arguments with reference to impoverished or lower-SES groups in general (Gottesman, 1968; Humphreys, in preparation). It should also be stressed that neither these psychologists nor Jensen holds any simplistic notion of race or of the association of skin pigmentation with intellectual capacity. Their point is simply that differential gene pools might exist for distinguishable groups of persons and that one cannot ignore the possible role of such factors in affecting capacities to learn.

The issue is a tricky one. At this point, it is not resolvable, but there are things that can and must be said in this regard. First, such heredity-vs.-environment questions do not exist only with reference to what we have called the "capacity to achieve." They exist with reference to all behavior. However, it is probably fair to say that, notably because of the cultural milieu in which most of us exist, the role of heredity and environment in determining intellectual development is especially salient. The heredity-vs.-environment issue is also socially and politically sensitive, and that fact probably does not help in the solution of the problem. Second, as in the case of most issues of behavior, it would be a mistake to look at the problem in terms of heredity *or* environment. The behavior we observe is always the result of an interaction of a certain hereditary potential within a certain experiential context. Indeed, it seems nearly impossible to assert that performance in any given case has been determined primarily by one factor or the other, and it seems foolish to try. Even the research of Jensen and others relates to *trends* among large groups and clearly reveals wide variability and overlap among these groups. Third, genetic theory would suggest that heritability factors will have appreciable effects in the case of identifiable groups when these groups exist within a stratified and open-class system (Gottesman, 1968). Thus, when factors other than heritable tendencies toward some kind of valued competence affect mobility among groups, the chances that a group's performance is determined by genetic factors are reduced. Slavery, discriminatory practices, and imposed economic conditions clearly do not allow for such mobility among groups. Finally, I am personally quite wary of inferring differences in competence when I see the ever-increasing amount of information that suggests the differential opportunity to learn. Even more telling perhaps is the work of the anthropologists who, every day it seems, uncover a finding which suggests that what we thought a child couldn't do, he in fact can do—if the setting and the context are right.

Is this heredity issue merely a racist thorn in the side of the body politic or is it an esoteric interest of an ivory-tower scholar here or there? My answer to both of these questions is no. While it seems most important to educators to give special consideration to the changeability of intellectual capacity, there is also danger in this. Uncritical optimism can lead to dashed hopes and extreme forms of reaction. There is some evidence of this in the United States at the present time, as inordinate promises of social reform through education have led to disillusionment with education in general. Those who seriously consider the degree to which intellect can change and the role of heritability factors in intelligence are not bigots or weird scientists. It is clear that they have served as a check on our optimism, and, insofar as unsupported optimism leads to disillusionment, they have played a positive role in the continuing discussion of culture and the capacity to achieve.

CHAPTER
FOUR
CULTURE AND
THE WILL TO ACHIEVE

Every teacher and every parent know that achievement is not just a function of intellectual capacity. There are times when the worst student does what we expect him to do. The child who can't finish an arithmetic assignment manages to make change and compute batting averages with ease. We know—or at least we think we know—that often children don't achieve simply because they don't want to, because it's not worth it to them, or because they have some "hang-up" about achievement. It is sometimes suggested that learning would inevitably occur if we could only get the child to *attend to* the task at hand. But how do you get children to attend to tasks? Why do some children show a clear enthusiasm for achieving situations while others avoid them?

These are interesting and important questions. Moreover, this line of questioning takes on special significance since it seems quite clear that "enthusiasm for achieving situations" has its origin in the child's socio-cultural background. Everyone knows that there is something wrong with the inner-city school or with the behavior that typically occurs there. Students are openly rebellious and seldom learn—that is, they seldom learn the prescribed and formalized aspects of the curriculum. Teachers despair, school boards organize investigations, and minority groups seethe with anger. Amidst the flurry of argument, discussion, charge, and countercharge that characterizes any important social problem, there are occasional sober suggestions regarding the causes of the very obvious dilemma. The suggestions, and probably also the causes, are many and varied. Classroom teachers usually exhibit an awareness of the problem and often have a profound appreciation of its complexity. They possess a special existential knowledge of the fact that many factors have created the dilemma that is the ghetto school. However, one aspect of the situation seems to be of special significance to teachers. Somehow there is something different about Sonny Suburb, who lives in a plush subdivision, and George Ghetto, who lives in the inner city. It isn't only that Sonny has cleaner clothes than George does or that Sonny more nearly shares the teacher's ways and words—although these differences are probably a significant part of the picture. The rewards and sanctions that seem to work with Sonny just don't seem to work with George. Somehow the carrot and stick that succeed in suburbia fail in the city's core. Sonny and George do not possess the same ability to work on their own, the same inclination toward academic pursuits, or the same motivation or will to achieve.

THE NATURE OF ACHIEVEMENT MOTIVATION

In a moment of euphoric irreality, I called this chapter "Culture and the Will to Achieve." To say the very least, the phrase "the will to achieve" is open to a variety of interpretations. Obviously, it reflects an interest in motivation. But what is meant by "motivation"? Who has it and how do we assess it? Where does it come from, and what does it do? Does it even exist? Before launching into an extended discussion of motivation, it might be well to pause and clarify the nature of the concept itself. What do we really mean when we say that a person is *motivated to achieve*?

When educators talk about motivation, we are often perplexed and sometimes disturbed by what we hear. Take, for example, the case of Sonny Suburb and George Ghetto. The conclusion that Sonny has a *desire* to learn and that George is not *motivated* is really quite unclear. Certainly, a desire or a motive is not something that can be directly observed. Perhaps one of the reasons why teachers and parents often disagree on the motives of children is that they are observing different things in making their judgments. Teachers and parents are not the only ones who differ on the question of motives. There is little unanimity among researchers and theorists either (see Cofer & Appley, 1964). That's not surprising. Even though man has probably always been interested in "motivational questions," the scientific study of these questions is of rather recent origin; it is probably best viewed as beginning with Freud (see Boring, 1950). Be that as it may, we have to begin somewhere, and we can best begin by looking at the aspects of *behavior* that prompt talk of motivation. Here we approach unanimity of opinion. Three different aspects of behavior typically evoke motivational inferences: activity, direction, and persistence.

The person concerned with understanding achievement is interested not so much in activity itself as in how that activity results in a specifiable outcome. Individuals vary in their output from situation to situation and place to place. When this variation in output cannot be attributed to other factors, such as changing competence, "motivation" usually is assumed to be the cause.

A second source of motivational inference exists in what might be termed the "direction" of behavior. In a classroom, while one student works at the assigned task, another may be exhibiting an equivalent amount of activity and output but of a different type and directed toward different ends. In such a case, we usually assume that the first student is more highly motivated.

However, either of these students may redirect his behavior at any given time. One way of conceptualizing this behavioral direction is to view the student as making a series of choices among behavioral alternatives. On the basis of the kinds of choices or decisions he makes, we may infer the motives that he possesses. Thus, the business of motivational theory and research is to predict the kinds of choices any given person will make among several alternatives.

In addition to the individual's preferred situation, behavioral patterns, and activities, the degree of his persistence in these activities also evokes a motivational explanation of his behavior. If a person continues to work on a series of problems when he could easily pick up a book, daydream, or converse with a classmate, we usually talk about his motivation toward the arithmetic task.

In general, *activity* or output level, *direction*, and *persistence* seem to be behavioral categories that elicit both formal and informal concern with motivation. The subsequent and critical question is: "what determines patterns of activity, direction, and persistence?" There are at least three different answers to that question, although they are in no sense mutually exclusive. These answers view the problem from the perspectives of personality, situation, and interaction between personality and situation. Together the three perspectives suggest a somewhat comprehensive picture.

PERSONALITY AND ACHIEVEMENT

The first answer to the question "what determines patterns of activity, direction, and persistence?" is diagramed as follows:

E $\longrightarrow$ P $\longrightarrow$ Achievement motivation
(early environment & (enduring & general (differential choice,
learning experiences) predispositions) persistence, and
performance)

Essentially what the diagram suggests is that certain formative experiences may shape persons quite differently from the way other experiences do as far as orientations toward achievement are concerned. Sonny Suburb and George Ghetto, for example, have been reared differently; they have been subjected to different sanctions and rewards, and they have been exposed to different ideologies, beliefs, and values. As a result, they have developed profoundly different personality patterns. If we ask why Sonny shows enthusiasm for achieving while George does not, the answer lies within the two individuals—what they are now as the result of their previous learning experiences. If we want to increase George's motivation, we must change *him*, reversing a history of previous learning and experience. Incidentally, that may be a bit difficult for a teacher to do!

SITUATION AND ACHIEVEMENT

Another possible answer to the question "what motivates?" resides in the *situation*. That is, the focus is on how different contexts, circumstances, and events may have a controlling influence on persons at any given moment, regardless of who the persons are or what their backgrounds might be. This answer is diagramed as follows:

$$S \text{ (situation)} \longrightarrow \text{Achievement motivation (differential choice, persistence, and performance)}$$

The emphasis here is not so much on previous background and enduring personality patterns—rather, it is on the pervading influence of immediate contexts. Achievement motivation or the lack of it depends on the situation. More or less implicit in this answer is the idea that anyone can be motivated, regardless of background, if we can identify and arrange for the appropriate conditions. More concretely, the whole matter of George's being enthused about school is not so much a problem that resides in him as it is a problem with the inner-city school, his teacher, or the immediate social context of the ghetto.

PERSON, SITUATION, AND ACHIEVEMENT

A third answer emphasizes the importance of both situation and person in analyzing the will to achieve. But there is more to it than that. This answer suggests that there are certain situations that optimize motivation in certain persons. The situation that motivates someone like George may have the exact opposite effect on Sonny. Motivation is a joint but interactive function of person and situation. To motivate, we must find the appropriate match between situation and person. We must assess the conditions that work best with certain individuals. Again, we might express this diagrammatically:

$$E \longrightarrow P \rightleftarrows S \; = \; \text{Achievement motivation}$$

(early environment & (enduring & general (situation)   (differential choice,
  learning   predispositions)   persistence, &
  experiences)   performance)

Note that the person and his previous background are not ignored. However, it is assumed that we can arrange for a situation that is most appropriate for each individual. Motivation is a matter of providing the proper match between situation and person.

CULTURE, PERSONALITY, AND ACHIEVEMENT

Certainly, the notion that achievement motivation is in some sense an enduring characteristic of the individual has validity. In the examples of Sonny and George, it does appear that Sonny reacts differently than George does in achieving situations because of experiences that have shaped the two boys differently. Many researchers have pursued this line of thought, but none have pursued it more tenaciously and productively than David McClelland and his colleagues and students (McClelland, Atkinson, Clark, & Lowell, 1953). Their work begins with an interest in assessment, continues with a dramatic example of cross-cultural research, and prompts most of the basic questions related to understanding the will to achieve.

DEVELOPMENT OF ASSESSMENT PROCEDURES

It was in the 1940s that David McClelland and his students became fascinated with the study of complex social motives. At the time, there was little systematic research on the kinds of motives that guide the behavior of people in complex situations. As a result, there was little agreement as to how motives should be defined. More important, there were few guidelines for measuring motives. Thus, at the outset, McClelland and his colleagues set for themselves the task of developing an appropriate assessment procedure. It does little good to talk about an *achievement motive* if it can't be measured. However, it is by no means an easy matter to translate some of our complicated, abstract, or, perhaps, just vaguely defined motives into operations that can be observed and indexed. How do we go about determining whether an individual has more or less achievement motivation? Obviously, that question is complex and multifaceted as well as important. A full discussion need not be presented here. It is sufficient for our present purposes to consider how McClelland and his colleagues dealt with the problem. Their solution is intriguing.

Following Freud's theories, McClelland and his associates initially assumed that motives exhibit themselves most reliably in a person's fantasy life. People's dreams, idle thoughts, and casual reflections on things and events were considered to be the best indicators of motives. Perhaps in these unguarded moments, a person's true self emerges. Perhaps thoughts that are very relevant to us and that have the greatest controlling influence on our affairs will most likely be exhibited when external constraints on our thinking are minimized. In any case, McClelland proceeded as if fantasy were the key to assessing motives, and he developed a standardized situation for eliciting fantasy samples from persons. Essentially, this procedure involved presenting an ambiguous series of pictures to an individual and asking him to make up stories describing what was going on. By design, the pictures were open to a variety of interpretations. What persons chose to see in the pictures probably depended on who they were and on what was on their mind. In other words, it was assumed that the stories would reveal something very basic about the persons writing them. Thus, if an individual were strongly motivated by an achievement motive, he would probably construct a story that would reflect this dominant theme in his life. If achievement were really an integral part of his personality, wouldn't this fact be revealed in an unguarded moment of fantasy? At least, we might expect that the stories of the highly achievement-oriented person would be measurably different from the stories of those who were minimally oriented toward achievement.

So the argument of McClelland and his colleagues went. And it does, I believe, make some sense. But how do we determine what kind of language, content, and imagery really represents an *achievement* orientation? To be sure, we might initially assume, on some sort of intuitive or common-sense basis, that certain types of expression and language reflect an achievement motive, but such common-sense assumptions are often wrong. McClelland and his colleagues were sensitive to this problem and decided not to depend entirely on what *seemed* to be achievement content. Rather, they set out to determine achievement content systematically and empirically. Their approach followed the pattern of experimentation designed to identify the nature and function of physiological drives, such as hunger. When an experimenter wishes to observe the variable effects of the hunger drive on behavior, he manipulates certain variables that presumably result in a hunger drive—that is, he usually places the organism on some type of food-deprivation schedule. When the organism has been without food for, say, 20 hours, it seems logical to conclude that it should have a stronger hunger drive than an organism that has just eaten. Similarly, differences in behavior in the two groups of organisms should be attributable to the hunger drive, all other factors being equal.

Although this approach may be quite acceptable in studying the hunger drive, it seems obvious that achievement is quite another matter. There is probably little disagreement on the approach of varying food deprivation in order to establish variation in the hunger drive. However, what do we manipulate in order to obtain variation in an achievement drive? This is indeed a perplexing problem, but McClelland and his associates did not shrink from it. Their approach was neither illogical nor unusual. Essentially, they asked subjects under different levels of achievement arousal to write stories in response to ambiguous pictures. In order to arouse the subjects' achievement motives, the researchers challenged them to do well at a task of some import. It was assumed that, if subjects were told that a task was a valid and important measure of their competence, they would be aroused to a greater degree than if the tasks were described as "experimental" and of low validity.

Such methods obviously differ from food deprivation as a means of producing a hunger drive, but it does seem likely that, if there is anything like an achievement motive, these routines should affect it. At least we might expect, even on an intuitive basis, that subjects would write different kinds of stories following such variations in achievement instructions. Moreover, it isn't difficult to agree with McClelland and his colleagues that any systematic differences in these stories are indicative of varying degrees of something that might be called an achievement motive. In any case, differences of several types were observed. They were categorized and noted, and procedures for scoring them were developed.

Since the method of analyzing the content is rather complicated and involved, it is difficult to describe it in detail here. The interested reader may pursue the matter by consulting the scoring manual that was developed (Atkinson, 1958). Suffice it to say that several criteria were considered in judging the degree of achievement motivation exhibited in a story. Among these criteria was the general theme of the story. Was it an achievement story? Principally, achievement means competition with some standard of excellence, but it also may involve a unique accomplishment or long-term involvement with attaining an achievement goal. Were any of these elements involved in the story? If they were involved, the evaluators noted the characters' relationships to these elements. Was an expressed desire to achieve attributed to the characters? Did they anticipate the accomplishment of some goal? Did the storyteller reveal how the goal would be reached? Were emotional reactions regarding success or failure in achievement attributed to the protagonists? McClelland and his colleagues assumed that the more clearly the storytellers expressed achievement themes and the more achievement elements they incorporated into their stories, the more they were likely to be dominated by an achievement motive.

Once the criteria and scoring procedures were developed, the researchers were prepared for the next significant step. If the tests were administered under "neutral" conditions—that is, under conditions in which no attempt was made to manipulate achievement motivation or to arouse an achievement orientation—individuals would doubtless vary in the kinds of fantasies they produced. According to the criteria for scoring achievement motivation, some would receive scores that were comparable to the kinds of scores received by subjects in the "aroused" condition of the experiment. Others would receive scores that were more nearly comparable to those received by subjects in the low-arousal condition. Given this possibility (indeed, observed fact), what use can we make of it? McClelland and his colleagues were quick to answer this question by assuming that individuals who received scores comparable to those received by subjects in the high-arousal condition possessed a more or less enduring personality trait predisposing them to achievement. Conversely, those who scored as the low-arousal subjects did were thought to be less achievement motivated.

If the pattern of assumptions and procedures followed by McClelland and his associates is valid, then the problem of assessing achievement motivation has been solved. We merely elicit fantasies from individuals and compare them to the stories produced by persons who were aroused for achievement and persons who were not. If the content, language, and imagery of an individual's fantasies more nearly approximate those of aroused persons, then he is logically termed "high" in achievement motivation. In shorthand fashion, he can be referred to as a "high-nAch person," where nAch is an abbreviation for *need* (for) *achievement.* If a person's fantasies are similar to the low-arousal pattern, then he is appropriately identified as "low" in achievement motivation ("low nAch").

McClelland's methods should ensure that this test has construct validity—that is, that it is related to achievement behavior. But perhaps another check on this might be desirable. Fortunately, subsequent research has provided a wealth of data designed to determine the construct validity of the assessment procedure developed by McClelland and his associates. Therefore, considerable information is also available on the characteristics of the high-nAch person. There is no mystery to what he prefers, likes, and typically does.

THE HIGH-nACH PERSON

It is somewhat of a fallacy, of course, to think of persons who are high or low in achievement motivation as separate personality types. Achievement motivation is presumably a continuous variable, and any division in terms of high and low is arbitrary. Thus, instead of asking "what is the high-nAch person like?" perhaps we should ask "with what other variables is achievement motivation correlated?" Be that as it may, much of the research has followed the practice of distinguishing between high- and low-nAch persons and observing the differences in behavior exhibited by groups of such individuals. Thus, in terms of the distinction made in the McClelland studies, it makes some sense to talk about different personality types. Besides, it is simpler to communicate what achievement motivation does by comparing clearly contrasting examples of the performance of individuals who represent extremes on the motivational continuum.

Thus, realizing that we are engaging in a convenient fiction, let's return to the question "what is the high-nAch person like?" We have identified high and low achievers on the basis of their fantasy life. For some persons, achievement seems to be a predominant response, an easily elicited theme, or something that is uppermost in their minds. Given half a chance, they think and talk about achievement. Fine and well, they dream great dreams, but do they *do* something? Once McClelland and his colleagues had devised a method for systematically scoring achievement themes, they proceeded to determine whether or not such dreaming was related to the complex behavior that is called achievement. Early research indicated that persons who exhibited a high degree of achievement fantasy did indeed show different achievement behavior than did those who showed little or no achievement imagery in their stories. For example, the "fantasy achievers," when given a choice, exhibited a clear preference for achieving situations. They seemed to welcome putting their competence on the line. "Fantasy achievers" also seemed to show an altogether different orientation toward achievement. They were likely to take a moderate risk in competitive and gamelike situations, seemingly welcoming a challenge. They were more likely to work on their own, with success at the task as the only reward. And, in general, they seemed willing and able to delay gratification and to work energetically and independently in order to live up to a standard of excellence. In short, they possessed the kinds of habits that would lead to achievement as well as an overall proclivity toward attaining success. Indeed, even the initial research efforts indicated quite clearly that the fantasy achievers were more than dreamers. They were doers as well. The fantasy measure was apparently a fairly good device for identifying persons who not only wanted to achieve but actually did achieve (McClelland, 1961; Heckhausen, 1967; Birney, 1968).

THE ACHIEVING SOCIETY

To have successfully identified a personality trait of relative stability and of some predictive value is no mean achievement. However, had the research stopped there, we probably would pay little attention to McClelland's accomplishment. Following the early preliminary work on the nature and assessment of achievement motivation, the research took an important new direction. A bold hypothesis was proposed that was concerned with the role of achievement motivation in bringing about economic growth.

It is quite obvious that societies and cultural groups differ in economic growth and general productivity. Moreover, we need only open a history book to become aware of the fact that each society waxes and wanes in this regard. Greece and Rome were mighty political, economic, and cultural forces at one time. They are hardly that today. Similarly, various societal groups, such as the southern Negro, the small-town white, or the suburban professional, exhibit differential degrees of drive and productivity. Why is this?

Part of the explanation undoubtedly lies in the variable opportunities presented to these groups as well as in their capacities to capitalize on them. Intuitively, it would seem that part of the explanation would also lie in the motivational realm. In *The Achieving Society,* McClelland (1961) gave this intuition some basis in empirical fact. Basically, McClelland's hypothesis was that a society shows economic growth when it fosters the development and the use of achievement-motivated persons.

In actuality, McClelland was proposing a variant of an older hypothesis originally suggested by the German sociologist Max Weber (1904). In *The Protestant Ethic and the Spirit of Capitalism,* Weber observed that Roman Catholic and Protestant European countries tended to differ in economic productivity and development, and he attributed this difference to the religious ethic espoused. Thus, he suggested that the "Protestant ethic" promoted self-reliance, denial of personal pleasure, and the evaluation of work as good in itself. Moreover, the emphasis on predestination presumably created some inclination for a person to establish himself as successful in order to achieve concrete, here-and-now assurance that he was indeed among "the elect." In short, Weber argued that the Protestant ideology led, if not inevitably at least rather directly, to capitalism and, more generally, to increased economic productivity.

McClelland suggested more specifically how ideology might result in a changed economy as well as in changed persons. The essence of McClelland's suggestion follows.

Protestant ethic   Economic
                                                                    productivity

            Achievement-oriented   Achievement-
            child-rearing practices   ─────────→   motivated persons

As can be seen from the diagram, this suggestion really consists of several hypotheses. First, it is hypothesized that each ideology fosters a certain characteristic pattern of child rearing and subsequently different kinds of personalities. That is, the Protestant ethic particularly emphasizes self-reliance, independent mastery, and individual competence. Assuming that Protestant parents indeed follow the accepted ideology in rearing their children, they should typically provide the ideal circumstances for creating highly achievement-oriented children. At least, there is some evidence (Winterbottom, 1953, 1958) that such achievement training is a precursor to an achievement orientation. Although parents may talk about achievement a great deal and establish it as a value, the important factor seems to be specialized achievement training rather than verbal and direct communication of an ideology. That is, as a child accomplishes something successfully and on his own, he acquires an increased interest not only in continuing to do that something but in attempting other tasks as well. There is a certain amount of uncertainty involved in attempting to do something you've never done before, to try a new thing, to master a new skill. Apparently, child-rearing practices can produce children who are oriented toward such risks as well as children who shrink from them. Thus, according to McClelland, child-rearing practices that emphasize independence training and mastery lead to high-nAch persons.

The next major assertion implicit in the McClelland theory is that, when ideology and practice favor achievement-motivated individuals to any important extent, a "spirit of capitalism" will result. This will tend to happen simply because there are more high-nAch persons contributing to the society. But this spirit is most likely to occur when these highly motivated persons are given the opportunity to fill leadership positions in the society. It is, of course, always possible that societal leadership may be vested in the hands of a low-nAch minority that does not allow participation from other than its own ranks. Thus, although there may be a sizable group of high-nAch persons, they may be prevented, at least temporarily, from exercising any controlling influence. Somehow, for a society to exhibit the spirit of capitalism in the sense of economic growth and productivity, the high-nAch persons must be allowed access to leadership positions.

This, in brief, is the hypothesis. It's intriguing to be sure, but does it have any basis in fact? How can we determine that achievement-motivated persons are the crucial element in a society's growth? Following the original analysis by Weber, we might categorize countries according to ideology and then measure their growth in some way. But how can the ideology of a culture be systematically identified, and how can growth be measured, especially in a way that takes some account of the fact that the opportunity for growth may not be the same in each instance? How do we systematically determine that achievement motivation plays an important role in this regard?

We might simply determine whether productive societies tend to have more achievement-oriented persons. But there is a problem here. If this relationship does exist, who is to say that there isn't really a third factor that causes both greater numbers of achievement-oriented persons *and* productivity? In other words, achievement motivation and productivity could be highly related without one necessarily causing the other, as illustrated here:

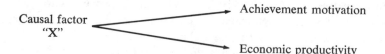

If we wish to establish that achievement motivation determines economic productivity, we should document achievement motivation in a society *before* economic productivity occurs. We should also be able to identify the relative nonexistence of achievement motivation in countries that continue to lack economic productivity. Suppose that we could arrange an experiment in which children in Germany, Japan, and Thailand would receive the kind of training that would result in high-nAch personalities, while children in Brazil, Italy, and Indonesia would not receive such training. Assuming that achievement motivation would exist only as the result of our training and only when we wanted it to, we should then expect, according to the McClelland hypothesis, that children in Germany, Japan, and Thailand would exhibit this particular personality trait to a greater extent than children in Brazil, Italy, and Indonesia. If achievement motivation is crucial for the economic growth of a nation, we should then also expect that, when these children become adults and take over the leadership of their countries, Germany, Japan, and Thailand would show greater economic growth than Brazil, Italy, and Indonesia.

Quite obviously, such an experiment is impossible. Another way to show that achievement motivation is a cause of economic growth is to perform what might be called a "naturalistic experiment." That is, instead of manipulating the causal variable directly, the researcher looks for instances in which it varies naturally, and he then attempts to isolate the effects. In the present case, it is conceivable that we could identify certain countries where achievement training is minimal and other countries where it is stressed. We could then wait until the children who were subjected to these different training experiences became adults and at that time compare the productivity of their nations. Few of us are patient enough to wait that long to determine whether our ideas have any merit. McClelland and his colleagues were no exceptions in this regard, and they introduced interesting methods that seem to adequately simulate such an experiment.

A first step in their procedure was to identify an index of economic productivity that somehow took account of the varying potential of the country. After considering several possibilities, two indexes seemed to be least objectionable. First, a procedure for comparing "real income" or purchasing power of the citizenry was employed. Second, electrical output of the country in kilowatt-hours was considered. Neither of these measures used separately is without flaw, but using both of them is one way of reducing error. However, even if these two measures do present a reasonably accurate picture of economic growth, a significant problem remains. Somehow, countries as well as people vary in their capacity to achieve. Certainly, in considering the economic growth of countries, we should not ignore the fact that one has rich ore deposits and another has none. Just as a teacher should take account of the ability of students in assessing achievement, so should the resources of nations be considered. And this is precisely what McClelland endeavored to do. On the basis of such information as coal production and level of development, he made a determination of the growth that could be expected of a nation. If a nation exceeded this prediction, it was considered an "overachiever"; if it fell below the predicted growth rate, it was considered an "underachiever."

Having arrived at a fairly acceptable way of identifying economic underachievement and overachievement, the next problem that had to be faced was one of assessing that all-important trait, achievement motivation. Remember now that the assessment of achievement motivation concurrently with the assessment of economic growth would not present a very convincing case that this personality trait or predisposition actually causes economic growth and productivity. The hypothesis states that it is the child-rearing practices experienced by the current industrial leaders that made them what they are—that is, either promoters or inhibitors of their country's economic progress. Thus, a primary cause of a present-day economic boom is the childhood experiences of the current leaders. It is easy enough to see how we could make an assessment of the economic productivity of a nation at any point in time, but how do we reach back into history to determine the shaping experiences that affected the leaders who are presumably responsible for this growth?

What McClelland did was to assume that the current leaders of any given country had been subjected to critical achievement training approximately 25 years earlier. He further assumed that the nature of this training could be most accurately indexed by considering the nature of classroom reading materials used during that earlier period. Such reading materials are usually available, for most highly developed societies at least, and it is relatively easy to analyze their content for achievement imagery, much as we would analyze the content of themes written in response to ambiguous pictures. Furthermore, it is probably not amiss to assume that stories in children's readers tend to reflect the behavior patterns that parents want their children to acquire. Most of us know what would happen if a book that was counter to parental wishes were to be made the required reading material for grade-school students. Through these textual materials, McClelland attempted to recapture the past experiences of the current leaders and to determine whether achievement was a dominant theme in their early training. He assumed that any correlation between reading materials of 25 or 50 years ago and current achievement would be difficult to attribute to a third factor, particularly if there were little or no correlation between current reading material and level of achievement. In other words, a naturalistic experiment with reasonable controls was simulated. The prime elements of this experiment appear in the following diagram.

INDEPENDENT OR CAUSAL VARIABLES	DEPENDENT OR RESULTANT VARIABLES
Child-rearing practices in 1925 (indexed by analysis of reading materials) ⟶	Economic growth of country in 1950
Presumed development of personality types – – – – – ⟶	Presumed existence of a society and societal leaders reflecting the ideology of the modal personality

An interesting feature of this simulated experiment is that there are many reasons why a correlation between the significant variables would not emerge. Wars, unusual climatic conditions, or discoveries of new resources, for example, could conceivably subvert any motivational tendencies created in the populace. Only McClelland's hypothesis, however, seems to explain why such a correlation *is* found. In extensive research, a positive relationship between child-rearing practices and economic growth was found, just as the hypothesis predicted. Furthermore, McClelland and his associates have continued to find such a relationship not only among a limited set of highly developed Western societies but among societies of almost every clime and time. There does indeed seem to be something to the notion that societies stand, fall, grow, or deteriorate as they attend to their children— that is, as they give them achievement training.

PERSONALITY AND ACHIEVEMENT: SOME CONCLUSIONS

DEVELOPMENT OF THE WILL TO ACHIEVE

From McClelland's work, it seems quite evident that personality can play a major role in achievement. Apparently, some individuals develop an achieving orientation very early in life, probably as the result of certain kinds of training or learning experiences. Moreover, it seems as if certain cultures and home environments provide these learning experiences to a high degree, while others do not (Adkins, Payne, & Balliff, 1972; Rosen, 1959; Zigler, 1970). But what is the explanation that the McClelland approach offers for the differential levels of achievement of Sonny Suburb and George Ghetto? The thrust of the McClelland research is that these two prototypes stem from different learning environments. Somehow Sonny Suburb has learned to want to achieve, while George Ghetto has not. There is, of course, considerable evidence that middle-class and lower-class homes typically differ in terms of facilitating the growth of achieving orientations (Proshansky & Newton, 1968). First, the middle-class family tends to foster values and an orientation toward life that directly and indirectly encourage achievement. In terms of the value dimensions discussed in Chapter Two, the middle class, in contrast with the lower classes, fosters an orientation to the future as opposed to the present or past and emphasizes doing as opposed to being or becoming (Kluckhohn & Strodtbeck, 1961). Such a future-doing orientation, along with direct and ever-present assertions that achievement is good, is certainly in part responsible for higher achievement tendencies in middle-class children.

Other factors are also likely to be involved. Sonny Suburb's family would also typically reinforce certain behavioral patterns that are instrumental to achievement. In accord with a futuristic orientation, the middle-class child, in contrast to his lower-class peer, typically learns to delay immediate gratification in order to gain larger future rewards. Therefore, he seems more oriented to symbolic as opposed to concrete material rewards

(Langer & Michael, 1963; Schneider & Lysgaard, 1953; Terrell, Durkin, & Wiesley, 1959; Zigler & Kanzer, 1962). Those behavioral predilections probably all play an important role in what the teacher comes to view as motivation to achieve. In addition, family dynamics and the role relationships of parents and children seem critical. Thus, the middle-class father is a fitting model for achievement, and his role is one in which he does not oppress the child's attempts to achieve competence on his own. This freedom for some initiative seems basic to the development of achievement motivation. A number of studies comparing child-rearing practices across widely divergent cultural groups have indicated that parental dominance is not likely to produce achievement-oriented children (Heckhausen, 1967, p. 150 *ff.*; McClelland, 1961, p. 345 *ff.*).

According to McClelland, there is at least one other critical factor. The child not only must be given an opportunity to learn basic achievement routines, to observe the right models, and to test his competence; he must also learn to *enjoy* accomplishing things on his own. This probably means that the child's independence should be encouraged at times and in situations when he is likely to succeed. Presumably, a child will learn to enjoy accomplishing things on his own—to achieve—if he is given freedom to attempt tasks that are not beyond his competence. This suggests that someone has to "program" the child's life in such a way that he is regularly challenged, but not challenged beyond his capacity to produce. That, of course, seems to be a role that middle-class mothers often play.

All in all, then, it is not too difficult to see how the personality-motivation hypothesis works out in the case of Sonny Suburb and George Ghetto. But, of course, the hypothesis is broader than these prototypes. Presumably, all of us experience achievement-motivation training to varying degrees, and we are accordingly more or less achievement motivated. As has been repeatedly implied, each person experiences his own social-psychological environment. That holds also for the aspect of the environment that is important in creating achieving orientations. Thus, Sonny Suburb's cousins or even his own siblings may not experience the same achievement training that he does. Indeed, when we say that achievement motivation is a function of personality development, we are also stressing this possibility of *individual* variation.

CHANGING ACHIEVEMENT PATTERNS

But what, if anything, can teachers and employers do about a will to achieve shaped largely by family and child-rearing experiences? Must they resign themselves to making the best of a bad situation in some cases and to being thankful for good fortune in other cases? Assuming that we want to increase an individual's motive to achieve, can we? In order to develop achievement-motivation patterns in persons, two courses of action are possible. We can attempt to do something about the early learning experiences that are presumably basic to the development of achieving orientations, or we can attempt to reverse these experiences by providing remedial training of some sort.

In the first course of action, then, child-rearing practices must be altered. Drastic economic and social changes may encourage families to change these practices. Thus, for example, if a father obtains an acceptable job—one that captivates his enduring interest and provides his family with basic subsistence needs—the achievement climate surrounding the children may also be altered. There is now a better model of achievement available for them to imitate. Perhaps the mother will have a greater opportunity to challenge her children, and perhaps their level of aspiration will be raised as the changing economic conditions provide new hope. But the word "perhaps" has to be stressed. Achievement models and appropriate aspirations and values are all important for the development of an achieving orientation. However, they do not appear to be the *sine qua non*. A specialized achievement training that fosters the successful confrontation of challenge and warmly rewards the independent mastery of tasks is at the basis of achievement motivation—at least as it has been studied by McClelland and his colleagues. Wealth does not necessarily ensure that parents will engage in this training. As a matter of fact, some studies indicate that the child-rearing practices of the upper classes actually discourage the development of achievement motivation (Strodtbeck, 1958; Rosen, 1962). Wealth merely provides the opportunity for parents to reflect on the art of child rearing, and it can give them the necessary freedom to become effective teachers of their offspring. Conceivably, social-intervention programs that assist mothers in rearing children could teach them how to motivate their children to achieve—if that is what they want to teach their children.

Although one should not rule out the possibility of changing achieving orientations by changing child-rearing practices, the success of this approach is uncertain at present. In changing achieving orientations, the second course of action—remedial training—has been primarily pursued. As a matter of fact, McClelland's more recent work has been especially devoted to this endeavor. One of the more fascinating projects that he attempted was the development of achievement-motivation training programs for business personnel in the United States and abroad. Surprisingly enough, the motivational pattern of relatively mature businessmen can be changed in such a manner that they become more productive and achievement oriented (McClelland, 1965a, 1965b; McClelland & Winter, 1969).

Basically, the program focuses on getting achievement thoughts to be dominant in the mind of the person. For example, one of the training routines consists of writing achievement themes. There are also opportunities to explore how to behave as an achievement-motivated person and to reflect on one's own potential in this regard. In other words, the program involves teaching as well as therapy. I, for one, am impressed with how the program participant learns to play a new role, much as the medical student must start to play a new role when he begins walking the wards.

Having had some success in changing the motives of business executives, McClelland has proceeded to operate on the assumption that the way to encourage the economic growth of a society is to select the leaders, train them in achievement motivation, and turn them loose in the appropriate positions. Perhaps the way to deal with underachievers in school is to initiate special extracurricular training programs. Several researchers have exhibited some success with such programs.

Employing approaches very similar to those that McClelland used with businessmen, Kolb (1965) ran a summer program directed toward the development of achievement motivation in underachieving high school boys. Again, the boys were taught what the high-nAch person was like. They were also given some practice in "thinking achievement thoughts" and in trying out the role of an achieving person—all in a reasonably accepting atmosphere. As one reads the description of what went on at the summer camp, it's difficult to refrain from suggesting that there was a good deal of role playing involved. That is, the boys were learning about and adapting to new expectations for themselves and were finding out that they could operate in this new way. At least in the case of boys from upper-socioeconomic-status families, the specialized training had the desired effects. A follow-up after a year and a half revealed that those students showed significant improvement in their grades. It is not altogether clear why lower-class students were not similarly affected. A reasonable guess, however, is that the subcultures in which the students held membership played critical roles. When reference groups do not provide continuing reinforcement of or support for the specialized training, its effects are ephemeral at best.

A FINAL STATEMENT

In sum, it does seem as if achievement motivation can be appropriately and productively viewed as a personality trait. Certainly, it makes sense to believe that something happens in childhood that may shape the will to achieve in an endurable manner. What is perhaps even more fascinating is that any effects of such early experience may be reversible. Even at a late age, human beings seem malleable with regard to basic character attributes. Missionaries, salesmen, and teachers have always hoped this to be true. It is reassuring to have empirical evidence that further justifies this hope.

CHAPTER
FIVE
PERSON, SITUATION, AND ACHIEVEMENT

More often than not, discussions of motivation focus exclusively on the person. It is assumed that there is something about or inside him or her that inevitably and unconditionally determines behavior. When I join my fellow faculty members for coffee, we sometimes talk about our colleagues—those who are absent, of course. From time to time, the conversation revolves around the accomplishments of this or that person and how he does it. Interestingly enough, I find that, in such informal conversations about achievement, behavioral scientists and humanists tend to use about the same explanations, if not the same language—that is, they say that "persons achieve because they are driven by some enduring internal force." Certainly, achievement does seem to be an enduring trait of individuals, and sociocultural experiences do seem to have a continuing influence on achievement, as emphasized in Chapter Four.

But the personality-achievement hypothesis cannot be the whole story. At best, it is an oversimplification; at worst, it is downright false. Complex human behavior is seldom if ever solely a function of the person. Achievement is no exception; it does not occur exclusive of certain situations and contexts. These situations and contexts are critical in eliciting or maximizing any predisposition to achieve. In some cases, situational factors may be more important than personality factors in determining achievement, but, in any case, we would do well to pay heed to how situations may or may not elicit a person's best efforts.

SITUATION AND ACHIEVEMENT

It is a general belief that certain teachers are "inspiring." As charismatic souls, they seem to have, be, or do something that invariably "turns students on." Likewise, it is thought that classroom or campus atmosphere may influence the will to achieve. Certainly, situations do seem to make a difference in what a person does, but what, more precisely, is it about a situation that prompts achievement? Apparently, there are many things—most of which are too elusive to identify here. However, there are several lines of inquiry that are especially intriguing in this regard.

GROUP MEMBERSHIP AND ACHIEVEMENT

Achievement does not occur in isolation from the individuals who are significant to us. As in the case of most behavior, in achievement, we are responding to the norms, values, and expectations of the groups that are significant in our world at a given moment. Our achievement therefore changes as our group membership changes. Most teachers are aware of this at a very functional level. During the middle grades, for example, the most resolute scholar may suddenly reject the values of the classroom for the glory of the ball field. Even if he continues to make good marks in the classroom, he will loudly and vociferously avow that he hates school, that teachers are dumb, and that schoolwork is not worth doing. The child who earlier was operating under the achievement norms, values, and expectations of adults—particularly of his parents and teachers—has now attached himself to another socially significant group, the peer group.

More often than not, the "lack of motivation" on the part of the ghetto child is a function of his membership in certain groups. It is the expectations, rules, rewards, sanctions, and aspirations of his peers that are critical in determining how he will approach achievement situations. Thus, Pettigrew (1967) points out that integration is important precisely because it establishes new and different social relationships and new groups with which the student can compare himself. When the black child is moved to a white suburban school, he is likely to confront a different normative structure as far as achievement is concerned. He is also likely to have a different social basis for judging his behavior. In other words, he experiences a different and perhaps better school, but, more significantly, he is likely to be forced into new social relationships. These new social relationships may be more important in changing his achievement patterns than the quality of the teaching or than anything else that happens in school.

At a general level, this is all fairly obvious. Yet the point is critical and must be emphasized. Persons—including children—identify with various groups. Groups of persons behaving together over a period of time evolve their own normative structures—that is, their accepted and approved ways of doing things. The more one group is isolated from another, the higher the probability that different norms, values, and expectations will evolve. That is fairly basic social science. It is also fairly important background to good teaching. In many cases, teacher and child are responding to different significant others, they are participants in different social groups, and their behavior is influenced by different norms, values, and expectations. As obvious as this may seem, it is interesting to observe that American educational systems typically ignore the role of peer groups in controlling behavior. More often than not, the classroom teacher assumes that he or she must control the behavior. By contrast, Russian educators are apparently more aware of the role of peer groups. They have invested considerable effort in developing procedures for effectively using the peer group in achieving adult-espoused objectives (Bronfenbrenner, 1970).

Achievement is a function of more or less ephemeral social expectations that are embodied in what we call norms. In a very real sense, a social group tells a person what to strive for as well as how to attain this end. The effect of such norms is clearly an important variable in any achieving situation. An exclusive interest in the person could make us forget the social constraints under which he operates. Perhaps the important and variable influence of social norms is best exhibited in a recent line of research on role expectations and achievement. Roles, as most social-science texts point out, are particularized norms or systems of norms. They are the systems of expectations that any group holds for persons occupying certain positions in a social system of some kind.

Before we get too bogged down in the abstract and perhaps irrelevant language of social science, let's consider several examples. Within most societies, there is a rather clearly designated role for "woman." This role varies from culture to culture, but norms are invariably associated with the position—that is, there is a way to be a woman. Interestingly enough, the way to be a woman may include achievement behavior that is quite different from the achievement behavior expected of men. Thus, McClelland describes achievement behavior that, in middle-class America at least, would typically be expected of men but probably not of women. The independent striving for mastery, the risk taking, the competitive pattern, and so on are not part of the female role. This is not to say that women do not achieve or exhibit these kinds of behavior; rather, it seems that the situations that elicit these actions on the part of men and women may be quite different (Horner, 1968, 1971; Rubovits, in preparation).

Consider the more fluctuating role of leader. Leaders change from day to day and sometimes from moment to moment. Zander and Forward (1968) found that, regardless of personality characteristics such as achievement motivation, subjects in their study exhibited the basic patterns of high-nAch persons when they were placed in a leadership role. Think of that: the momentary shift from follower to leader apparently "motivated" subjects to act like high-nAch persons. Perhaps achievement motivation is really just a matter of learning this or that social role and playing it when the social situation demands it.

Such an interpretation would place major weight on the role of social situations in determining the will to achieve. Several studies of the effects of social role and status on achievement (see Klinger & McNelley, 1969) show that this interpretation cannot be lightly pushed aside. One of the strong implications of this line of research is that children from the lower classes do not achieve at the rate of those from the upper classes simply because they are not expected to do so—by teachers, by peers, or even by their parents. The importance of such expectancies in conditioning achievement should not be underestimated. To a surprising extent, children fulfill prophecies about themselves. They become what we expect them to become, and they play the roles we assign to them.

TEACHER AND SITUATION

Since situations do affect achieving patterns, is there any way that the teacher can create situations that will facilitate achievement? That question is probably troubling you, especially if you are, or are about to become, a teacher.

In attempting to deal with this question, let's start where we left off in discussing situations and achievement. An important part of any achievement environment must be the implied or stated expectations that exist for those who participate in that environment. If a school or classroom is run under the assumption that the students won't amount to much, chances are they won't. Probably teachers can play some role in manipulating the expectations that children hold for one another. Perhaps they can infiltrate the peer group and effect change in the norms that students hold for themselves. Occasionally, an especially charismatic teacher may do this—*how*, we're not at all sure. Furthermore, the teacher himself can hold different expectations for students, and these expectations may indeed be a crucial aspect of any classroom situation. This seems clear from a remarkable series of studies on what has come to be called the *Pygmalion effect*.

Anyone who has seen or read about *My Fair Lady*, or the play by George Bernard Shaw on which it was based, knows something about the Pygmalion effect. Both the play and the musical involve a clear case of one person changing another by teaching and training but, above all, by expecting that person to change. Professor Higgins wagers that he can make a gentile lady out of an uncultured cockney lass and does. It is not quite as amazing as the original myth, in which the sculptor Pygmalion falls in love with his statue and thereby brings the work of art to life. Yet in both cases, expectations make a difference.

In *Pygmalion in the Classroom,* Rosenthal and Jacobson (1968) report an interesting study of the effects of teacher expectations. The study was simple enough in design and execution, but the results were nothing short of astounding. At the beginning of the school year, students took a test that presumably identified those who were "intellectual bloomers"— that is, those who were about to exhibit a spurt in intellectual development. The teachers were then told that they could expect substantial intellectual growth from particular students during the course of the year. Thus, teachers were given the expectation that certain students would show increased achievement as the year proceeded while others would not. In actuality, of course, the test was only a standard intelligence test, and the information given to the teachers was not based on the test at all. Rather, the researchers selected potential "bloomers" on a purely random basis regardless of actual intellectual potential. Nevertheless, the children labeled as "bloomers" exhibited the intellectual growth predicted of them; more accurately, they exhibited greater I.Q. gains than their classmates did. It seems that the prophecy was fulfilled simply because it had been made. When teachers were led to believe that students would show increased intellectual growth, the students did show such growth! Probably because the results are so amazing, this study has been submitted to many and varied criticisms (Elashoff & Snow, 1970; Finn, 1972; Minor, 1970; Snow, 1969; Thorndike, 1968, 1969), and the findings have not always been replicated (see, for example, Claiborne, 1969). However, it does seem that Rosenthal and Jacobson were on to something. After all, this is only one of many studies that seem to point in this direction (see, for example, Rosenthal, 1966).

But even if the existence of a Pygmalion effect is granted, how does it occur? How do the expectations of a teacher transfer to the child in such a way that his behavior is changed? Studies by Rubovits and Maehr (1971, 1973, in preparation) suggest rather clearly that, when teachers expect certain things from their students, they tend to behave toward them in ways that are demonstrably different from the ways in which they behave toward other students. That is, teachers show a qualitatively different treatment of presumed "gifted" and "nongifted" students; they engage in behavior that one might expect would encourage or motivate those who are labeled as "gifted." They reward more, criticize less, and generally encourage the child to live up to what they *believe* possible for him.

All in all, then, it is quite apparent that the beliefs of teachers— their expectations for students—are among the most crucial aspects of a classroom environment. When a teacher believes that a child from the ghetto or pueblo *can't* achieve, the teacher's behavior seems to ensure that the child won't achieve. When the teacher believes the child *can* achieve, a totally different situation seems to exist. People are controlled by their thoughts. Their interactions with others are controlled by how they view these others, and that is basically what is involved here.

CLASSROOM ATMOSPHERE

Teachers' expectations for their students are an important aspect of any achievement situation. However, there are other aspects of the learning situation that may be equally if not more important. One of these is classroom atmosphere.

Different classrooms are characterized by different atmospheres; they even look different to the casual observer. One is busy and noisy; another is well ordered and quiet. In one, the teacher is obviously the central figure; in another, students seem to initiate much of the activity. But what about these many and varied conditions? Are they good, bad, or indifferent as far as achievement is concerned? That question has been hotly debated over the years with little real outcome. It has also been researched to some extent but with little success in arriving at a viable conclusion.

Recently, there has been much emphasis on creating a classroom atmosphere in which the student has considerable autonomy. Of course, it is fully recognized that the nature of the classroom environment must be varied according to the age of the students, but the goal is to treat each child humanely and, above all, with respect for his considerable potential. That usually involves giving him what appears to be an increased amount of freedom in the learning situation. External evaluation is minimized—especially as a motivator for performance—and it is typically assumed that the child is, for the most part, intrinsically motivated to learn. Teachers are told that if they provide him with the right resources, the child will learn in his own time and way—without the imposition of threats or promises. Above all, teachers are instructed to refrain from using *group-* based standards and norms as frames of reference for any actual or implied threats or promises. The child is to be viewed on his own terms. Therewith, he must also be given a chance to choose between alternatives and to select what he will or will not do. If a choice of tasks is precluded, he must be able to do the task in his own way. The essence of autonomy is choice or the perception that one has choice. The child must be thought of as the determiner of his own behavior—not as an object of instruction but as the one who is learning!

But how does such autonomy affect the motive to achieve? Although that is a difficult question to answer definitively, it is possible to come up with bits and pieces from diverse projects that seem to yield an acceptable but tentative answer. Richard deCharms (1968, 1972) has pursued a provocative line of inquiry here.[1] Basically, deCharms has argued that when a person feels that he is the *origin* of his behavior and the controller of his fate, he acts quite differently than when he feels that he is simply the *pawn* of other persons, things, or events. Thus, deCharms reinterprets achievement motivation in origin-pawn terms, suggesting that the highly motivated person is one who perceives himself as responsible for the outcome in achieving situations and who views situations as under his control. When an individual interprets a situation in such a manner, he behaves quite differently than when he views it as beyond his control. Specifically, he appears more highly motivated. He works harder and more effectively and persists at tasks for longer periods.

There are several lines of evidence that provide support for the basic origin-pawn notion. Among them is the Coleman Report (1966), which indicated that the best predictor of school success was a fate-control variable. Thus, if children felt they were in control of their worlds, they were more likely to be successful in school. But the Coleman Report really only *suggested* that an individual's acceptance of personal responsibility for his achievement or a person's belief in his ability to control his world is at the root of achievement. It did not clearly rule out the possibility that those who, for one reason or another, just happen to achieve also just happen to feel they are responsible. It is at this point that deCharms' work begins to take on its fullest meaning. Basically, what deCharms did was to show that certain kinds of conditions will not only lead to different perceptions of personal control but will also significantly change an individual's performance. Thus, it seems that when the individual is treated as the *origin* of his behavior—as one who is engaging in an act on his own terms—he then exhibits increased motivation. Therefore, classrooms or other situations that lead a person to believe that he is responsible for his performance should increase motivation.

But what kinds of situations might prompt such a feeling of personal control, and, more precisely, how would motivation be affected? At least two kinds of situational factors would probably tend to increase the origin feeling: (1) freedom from external evaluation and (2) freedom to choose among alternatives. Moreover, the maximization of freedom in these ways increases performance level, at least in certain situations and for certain kinds of persons. Thus, Menz (1970) found that gifted and presumably highly motivated college students performed at a higher level when

---

[1] The interested reader may also wish to consider Weiner's (1972) interpretation of achievement motivation in terms of attribution theory.

they were given a choice of tasks than they did when they were assigned a task.

Of equal if not of greater interest is the effect of such freedom on what might be called "continuing motivation." What the student does in the classroom is important, but perhaps of greater importance is what he does outside the classroom. Thus, in actuality, it may be of prime interest that the child somehow be stimulated to continue classroom-related activities outside the classroom. In my experience, teachers point with special pride to the student who spontaneously pursues a course of study that was merely introduced in a classroom situation. That is supposedly *real* motivation and a highly valued educational outcome. It is this tendency or predisposition to continue working at a task or to attempt, on one's own, new but related tasks that we refer to as "continuing motivation."

In this regard, a preliminary study by Maehr and Stallings (1972) is of interest. In this experiment, subjects performed tasks under two different evaluation conditions. The external-evaluation condition simulated a typical classroom situation in which subjects were led to believe that their performance would be evaluated and that the results would be made known to their teachers as well as to themselves—that is, the tasks were described as a kind of test. In the internal-evaluation condition, subjects were led to believe that their level of performance was really "their own business." Although they were given feedback on the number of right and wrong solutions to the various problems posed, it was emphasized that the experimenters were not interested in their performance per se, only in their subsequent rating of the interest value of the tasks. It was also stressed that teachers would not be informed of the results and that students should do the tasks in a spirit of fun.

Contrary to what one might expect, external evaluation did not necessarily motivate students to perform at a higher level. Of special interest, however, was the way in which "continuing motivation" was apparently affected. Whereas external evaluation seemed to prompt students to return to tasks on which they had been successful and to avoid tasks on which they had failed, a different tendency was noted under internal-evaluation conditions. When students worked on tasks under the internal-evaluation condition, they were likely to avoid returning to an easy task— one on which they could be reasonably assured of continued success. Instead, they exhibited a preference for returning to and working on a task at which they had not succeeded. Thus, reduced external evaluation seemed to stimulate, or at least allow for, a tendency to confront challenge—to do that which was difficult and for which the outcome was uncertain. However, it is important to add that this tendency was most clearly evident in achievement-oriented students—in this case, students of junior-high age.

Along a similar line, Thornes (1971) conducted an experiment in which some subjects performed under relatively free conditions and others under conditions of relative restraint. More specifically, the free subjects were led to believe that they had some choice in what they would do and that their level of performance was a matter of only their own concern. The remaining subjects were *assigned* their task and were pointedly informed that their performance would be evaluated by teachers as well as by the researchers giving the "tests." In a fashion somewhat parallel to the Maehr-Stallings study, high-achievement-oriented students showed greater continuing motivation under the relatively free-performance conditions.

The evidence is just beginning to accumulate, but it does seem that a learning environment that is characterized by relative autonomy may result in important desired outcomes, particularly for students who are intrinsically motivated to achieve. That, of course, is not a new message, and, in one sense, it is a message that is being promoted by individuals concerned with "opening up" the schools. However, these data seem to add at least a nuance or two to the message. First, they suggest some ways in which we might conceptualize openness and freedom in order to identify specific effects on behavior. Quite frankly, it is my opinion that much of the talk about openness and freedom in education has been excessively vague. Certainly, the propositions espoused by educational reformers arguing for such openness have not been open to test by accepted scientific methods. Secondly, these studies also seem to call attention to an oft-forgotten but nevertheless critical educational outcome: continuing motivation. Most studies of educational experiences focus on rather immediate performance outcomes. Since individuals rapidly forget much of what they learn in or through any educational experience, perhaps it is well to emphasize the development of a continuing interest on the part of students to recall, review, and generally enhance their educational experiences—on their own. In this regard, an open educational environment may be of value because it has important effects on *continuing* motivation to learn and to perform.

But in all of this, a nagging question remains. Such openness or freedom as was evident in the cited studies seems to be the most effective for certain kinds of persons. Apparently, the effect of freedom (or perhaps any other environment) on behavior is always specifically dependent on the person. It is to the question of how certain environments may have differential effects on certain kinds of persons that we now turn.

INTERACTION OF PERSON AND SITUATION

It is difficult not to qualify each assertion about the effects of situations on motivation with a reference to individual differences. Apparently most situations affect persons differently as far as achievement is concerned. It also appears that this individual variation is significantly affected by early social experiences, some of which are culturally determined. Although that greatly complicates educational planning, it is not something that can be easily ignored. Therefore, we must give special consideration to the interaction of person and situation when we attempt to understand the sociocultural origins of motivation.

Without doubt, anyone can identify a great many situations that seem to affect persons differently. But when we examine this long list, several facets of situations seem to emerge as preeminent. These are (1) the level of challenge presented by the situation, (2) the degree to which the individual structures the situation for himself, and (3) the mode by which success and failure are communicated.

INDIVIDUAL DIFFERENCES IN RESPONSE
TO CHALLENGE

John W. Atkinson brought a number of different lines of thought together and provided an initial but enduring statement on the interaction of individual achievement orientations and different environments. There are many intriguing aspects to this statement, several of which are especially important here. According to Atkinson, when a person confronts an achievement situation, two competing tendencies are aroused in him to a greater or lesser degree. He is attracted by the possibility of success, and, simultaneously, he is fearful of the possibility of failure and is motivated to avoid it. Think back for a moment on a career or curriculum choice that you have made and consider whether or not fear and hope were both involved as you puzzled over what to do.

For Atkinson, achievement is a function of these two ever-present and competing tendencies, which seem to exist in individuals to a greater or lesser degree as a kind of personality characteristic. One person might be more dominated by the expectation of success and another by the fear of failure. The relative strength and pervasiveness of these predispositions seem to result from different socialization contexts. Thus, for example, it is conceivable that parents may focus special attention on a child when he fails and may show little response when he succeeds. Conversely, they may mollify the hurt of failure or choose to make little of it and may give primary attention to the child when he succeeds. In short, some children are blamed more for failing, while others are praised more for succeeding. Many disadvantaged children seem bound to fail in certain situations, whereas other children seem "programmed for success." This conflicting orientation to achievement—whatever its precise origin—appears to be a personality variable similar to McClelland's concept of nAch. It is a predisposition that a person brings to any given situation.

But motivation, for Atkinson, does not stop with the person. It is always a combination of both personality and situational factors. That is, each person will come to the achieving situation with a greater or lesser tendency to succeed or avoid failure. The relative strengths of these tendencies vary with the individual. However, the situation will play a critical role in determining how the tendencies are actualized in behavior. In considering the situation, Atkinson focuses primarily on the probability of success or failure, or what might more generally be termed the *challenge* of the situation. Is the achievement task easy, difficult, nearly impossible? According to Atkinson, persons with varying achievement orientations will respond quite differently to variations in challenge. Generally speaking, the person who is oriented toward success will be most highly motivated when the task is challenging. When either success or failure is virtually assured, the success-oriented person's motivation is reduced. The reverse is true for the failure-threatened person. He is most highly motivated when uncertainty and challenge are reduced. Whether the outcome is success or failure, he prefers it to be predictable. Another way of stating this is to suggest that the success-oriented person is typically interested in testing his competence and that he probably expects to enhance his self-regard with a new accomplishment. The failure-threatened person, however, resists any test or evaluation of his competence, and therefore he will choose the predictable. Even predictable failure is preferred to challenge. After all, choosing to work at an impossible task or at an easy one is one way of avoiding any serious confrontation with one's competence or lack of it.

The motivational patterns suggested by Atkinson's formulation are summarized and presented pictorially in Figure 5.1. As you might guess, behavior does not always pattern itself as neatly as Figure 5.1 indicates. But the hypothesis expressed there has received substantial support (Atkinson & Feather, 1966; Maehr & Sjogren, 1971). This rather general "challenge hypothesis" provides a productive perspective on various educational processes. Its application to the problems of ability groups and of learning materials and tasks will be presented here. A fuller discussion can be found elsewhere (see Maehr & Sjogren, 1971; Weiner, 1967, 1970, 1972).

Ability Grouping

Ability grouping is found in some form in most classrooms. Even in an ungraded-primary or one-room school, similar-ability reading and math groups are created. The real purpose of such arrangements may be to ease the teacher's task, but, nevertheless, it is important to inquire into the

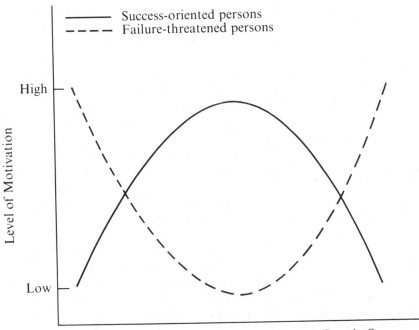

Figure 5.1. Theoretical motivational patterns of success-oriented and failure-threatened persons.

effects such grouping has on children. First of all, it is doubtful that ability grouping by itself necessarily has a positive effect on achievement (see Schafer & Olexa, 1971). However, ability grouping may affect different persons in different ways. Atkinson's model suggests that this is indeed the case. The model has been used to make predictions about the performance of persons with different achievement orientations in ability-grouped classrooms. It seems likely that ability grouping will affect the level of challenge that is typically presented to the child. Overall, in an ability-grouped classroom, each child should be more realistically challenged—that is, each child should have a better chance of competing for whatever rewards may be available. In a classroom where there is a wide ability spread, however, some children are inevitably doomed to failure and others are assuredly destined for success.

If it is true that ability-grouped classrooms present a realistic level of challenge for a greater number of students than do classes that are not ability-grouped, then Atkinson's model makes some rather specific predictions about the situation. The model does not predict that ability grouping itself will have an overall effect on all children. Rather, it suggests that motivation will be increased for those persons who are characterized by relatively strong orientations toward success. Conversely, individuals who are dominated by a fear of failure will actually exhibit a reduction in motivation. Challenging situations are a matter of some discomfort to them, and, if they cannot avoid these situations, they will perform only at a minimal level. Thus, ability grouping may be a good way to motivate students who are oriented toward success, but it won't work for students who operate primarily in response to a fear of failure.

Unfortunately, this intriguing hypothesis has had only minimal testing. However, at least one major study (O'Connor, Atkinson, & Horner, 1966) has been concerned with this point. The results of this study were more or less in line with the hypothesis. Success-oriented students exhibited greater growth in academic achievement and more interest in schoolwork when they were members of an ability-grouped class. While failure-threatened students did not actually exhibit a difference in performance that was attributable to class grouping, they nevertheless showed less interest in schoolwork when they were placed in an ability-grouped class. In terms of continuing motivation, the effects of grouping on the interest level of success-oriented and failure-threatened students are perhaps the most interesting finding here. In any case, this major study, as well as some other lines of evidence, suggests strongly that it is not amiss to consider achievement orientation as a critical variable in grouping students (see also Smith, 1969). Moreover, we can logically go beyond these results to hypothesize that cultural groups that characteristically exhibit different achieving orientations may be affected differently by grouping procedures. Thus, for example, the middle-class child, who more characteristically exhibits a success orientation than the disadvantaged child does, may be expected to benefit more from ability grouping.

Learning Materials and Tasks

Atkinson's model of motivation patterns can also be applied to the selection of appropriate educational materials and tasks as well as to techniques in teaching. The model suggests that regular and consistent success is not likely to motivate the success-oriented student. However, consistent success may be precisely the situation that is most desirable for the failure-threatened person. Thus, we might expect, for example, that programmed-learning materials, which are designed to ensure that the student seldom fails to get the right answer, would be best suited for the failure-threatened individual. Indeed, this expectation does seem to be warranted (Maehr &

Sjogren, 1971). But more generally, it seems that learning materials and techniques that are based on the principle that all children should receive a maximum of success are not automatically going to solve motivational problems. As a matter of fact, it seems clear that the achievement-oriented student may be motivated by the very possibility of failure. Whereas he is bound to become bored by repeated success, failure or the probability of failure is necessary to retain his attention and elicit his performance. Again, it is possible that different cultural groups will *tend to* include persons with different achieving orientations. Therefore, the teacher might expect "challenge" and "assurance" to be differentially effective with children from diverse cultures.

INDIVIDUAL DIFFERENCES IN RESPONSE TO FREEDOM

The Atkinson theory illustrates how challenge interacts with personality in determining motivation. Challenge, it may be agreed, is at least one readily identifiable and important aspect of any achievement context. Another crucial component is freedom, or the degree to which the person is allowed to structure the achievement situation for himself and on his own terms. Earlier it was noted that freedom and constraint variously characterize any given classroom. It was also implied that such situational conditions will have differential effects on individuals—that is, what freedom will do for one person, it won't do for another. Thus, in the studies cited, not only did the atmosphere of freedom have an important general effect on achievement, but, to an important degree, it also had special effects upon individuals characterized as high or low in achievement orientation. Apparently, it is the highly motivated student who benefits most from freedom. This suggests that the effectiveness of independent study, with minimum emphasis on grades and maximum choice for the student, depends significantly on the student's *motivational* orientation. From a slightly different theoretical perspective, David Hunt (1971) has emphasized that students vary in the degree to which they can structure situations for themselves and therefore vary in the degree to which they benefit from autonomy. Moreover, those working with Hunt on what has been termed *conceptual systems theory* have been able to identify individuals who will and who will not respond positively to relatively unstructured environments. Subsequently, they have experimented with grouping procedures that allow each individual to benefit from the learning environment most appropriate for him.

Of course, all of this is quite preliminary and experimental. However, there is an intriguing possibility that researchers with a variety of theoretical commitments may well be converging on one major issue: the capacity for independence in learning. We usually assume that the *intellectually* gifted student should have freedom but that others would benefit more from an imposed structure. However, motivational orientation, not intelligence, is probably the key to who will benefit most from learning environments that increase the responsibility of the student. This is the message that can be derived from the research thus far. Moreover, it is an extremely relevant message in view of the current emphasis on openness in American and British education. It is scarcely less relevant in considering education in Ghana, Afghanistan, or Thailand. One of the perennial problems in certain cultural contexts is to get students involved, in an independent way, in learning. The converging interest in the independence-dependence orientation may well force researchers to seek out the sociocultural origins of these learning modes with a view to changing them and/or to adapting education accordingly.

But this is saying very little about what is obviously an important issue today in education. The effectiveness of open classrooms, no-fail systems, and student-structured learning programs in some sense will probably depend on a fuller understanding of the motivational issues involved, and that fuller understanding is not to be had as yet. For now, we simply have some suggestions and the promise of a line of research.

INDIVIDUAL DIFFERENCES IN RESPONSE TO FEEDBACK MODE

In any achievement situation, there are a variety of modes by which success can be communicated. Success and achievement may be expressed by a person and may be accompanied by varying degrees of warmth. The task itself may indicate success—for example, success is indicated when a puzzle is solved. And, there are doubtless other possibilities. Moreover, success can be communicated directly and without delay, or it may initially appear in the form of a promise of greater things to come. These various means of communicating success are not equally effective for each individual, and research has suggested several interesting patterns of feedback effectiveness.

Following up on the line of study initiated by McClelland and Atkinson, researchers have obtained several findings of major interest. In an early study conducted by French (1958), it was found that individuals high in achievement motivation (nAch) and individuals high in affiliation motivation (nAff) responded differently to different expressions of success.

Subjects in French's study worked in small teams on a task that required group participation and cooperation to assemble a story from various isolated phrases. The feedback was either achievement-oriented ("this team is working very efficiently") or affiliation-oriented ("this team works very well together"). The teams whose members were characterized by high achievement motivation worked best with achievement-oriented feedback, while teams high in affiliation motivation worked best with affiliation-oriented feedback. In brief, it seemed that maximum effort was elicited from subjects when the feedback matched their motivational orientations. More generally, this and other studies have indicated that the high-nAch person is more oriented toward feedback that is clearly tied to achievement—that is, he prefers being right or correct as opposed to gaining approval or earning extrinsic rewards. He is interested in achievement for its own sake and responds accordingly.

The satisfaction of being correct does not seem to be a sufficient incentive to spur socially disadvantaged children on to greater heights. But even within the typically achievement-oriented middle class, different personality trends emerge, and a mode of feedback can have differing effects. Clearly, teachers must be discerning enough to apply differential reinforcement-feedback patterns to elicit maximum efforts from their students. From work related to achievement motivation as well as to other approaches (see Stuempfig & Maehr, 1970; Zigler, 1970), it is apparent that the person from a lower socioeconomic stratum in our society responds more favorably to the less abstract achievement feedback and works best for concrete rewards, including the clear demonstration of approval by a significant other. But how does a person's "culture of origin" predispose him to differential reward structures? This is a provocative question, and one for which only a few sketchy answers have been offered.

PERSON AND ENVIRONMENT:
AN IMPORTANT AFTERTHOUGHT

What emerges from this discussion of situation and person is that achievement environments can vary, and, as they vary, they have differential effects on individuals. The environment referred to, of course, is a psychological environment—an environment composed principally of social interactions, personal control, perceived opportunities, and other aspects of interpersonal relationships that typify all social and most educational situations. Clearly, this implies that effective teaching will involve matching the right environment to the right person. But even if we had a complete knowledge of environments and persons—which obviously we do not—

there would still be a major problem in applying our knowledge. It is all well and good to say that each child should be treated as an individual. It is fine to say that some children should be challenged and others encouraged. And indeed, it would be helpful to have a good means for determining more specifically who should be treated in what manner. But the teacher is confronting 30-plus students and is attempting to reach all of them more or less simultaneously. As a result, the teacher is most likely to ask what he or she can do in managing the group or the classroom environment that will be most effective—if not for all at least for most students. Is there any way that the teacher can effectively fit the environment to each person?

Perhaps this is in a very real sense an implicit plea for the individualization of instruction. Recently developed self-instruction devices and materials, some of which are adaptable to motivational differences as well as to intellectual differences, might be helpful. If many of the routine teaching tasks could be left to automated and/or self-instructional devices, the teacher could be freed to be more of a clinician, to deal individually with the learning problems of each student, and to bring the most effective incentives to bear in each case. That is a possibility and certainly one worth keeping in mind. It is probably a realistic possibility only for school systems that have ample resources. After all, most instructional materials that relieve the teacher of certain tasks do cost money if, indeed, they are even available for purchase. It would be totally ridiculous to encourage the typical Education Corps teacher in Iran to individualize instruction in this manner and to advise him to play the role of the clinician. The materials for such pedagogy would simply not be available, and such an approach would probably not be an acceptable notion within the culture.

There may, of course, be other ways of enabling the teacher to be more of a clinician. English schools are not characterized by low teacher-student ratios, yet some very interesting styles of teaching have emerged there that seem to allow for a bit more individualization of instruction without the aid of expensive automated-instruction devices. The classroom has been opened up. Children are given an autonomy to pursue a variety of activities with minimal regimentation, more or less according to their own schedule. Although the teacher may be in charge of as many as 40 children at a time, the students are free to pursue a variety of interests on their own. The role of the teacher as the person who imparts knowledge has been minimized. Instead, the instructor sets the scene, serves as a consultant, and, potentially, may individualize the level of challenge. There is too little known about these open schools to really be sure that such a clinical role on the part of the teacher is possible except in unusual cases. However, this is indeed a possibility worth exploring further.

A more obvious or at least traditional way of matching personality and environment might be to employ some variant of homogeneous grouping. As suggested previously, there may be some value in taking a personality trait such as achievement motivation, as well as intelligence, into account in grouping students. The teacher could then behave rather consistently and effectively on the assumption that her students need certain kinds of learning environments, learning conditions, teacher responses, and so on. In any case, it seems reasonable to consider differential achieving orientations as well as intelligence in grouping procedures.

When a teacher conducts a class, he or she not only communicates information but also creates an achievement environment of one kind or another—a psychological world for the student that may have differential effects on his motivation. Although we have just begun to explore the dimensions of such psychological environments, we can at least fairly readily determine some factors that encourage or discourage different kinds of students. Some achievement environments stress achievement in and of itself, allow for considerable independence, and regularly present a challenge. Such environments are probably most effective with certain kinds of students. Some achievement environments may stress affiliation, compatibility, and support and may reduce challenge. These environments are also effective with some students but not others.

In summary, then, we know a little bit about the kinds of person-situation matches that allow maximal achievement—probably enough to justify experimenting with assigning persons to differential teaching environments depending on their achievement orientation. But whether or not we can justify engineering these person-environment matches, an important point remains. In the final analysis, motivation is a function of both person and situation. There are few universally effective ways of motivating children. Children who differ in sociocultural background will likely differ in response to the motivators employed in school. Somehow the teacher must fit the situation to the person in order to maximize student effort—and that is creative teaching!

CHAPTER
SIX
A CONCLUDING CAVEAT

The typical middle-class teacher is often accused of racism. Perhaps this charge has already been made against you. If not, it soon might be. The accusation is a most serious one—one that cannot be lightly dismissed. However, it is difficult if not impossible to assess the validity of such an accusation. Racism is a loaded word that is difficult to define to everyone's satisfaction. Possibly, however, the typical teacher does behave in one way with children who share his or her culture and in quite a different way with those who do not. This would not be surprising, since that is how most people tend to behave. But do teachers discriminate in such a way that they tend to reduce the chances that children from cultural groups other than their own will succeed?

With a view to answering this disturbing question, Pam Rubovits and I (Rubovits & Maehr, 1973) pulled what can only be described as a "dirty trick" on some prospective teachers. Our trick was based on the work on teacher-expectancy effects done by Rosenthal and Jacobson (see Chapter Five) and was designed to carry this line of research a step or two further. In addition to considering teacher-expectancy effects in a rather general way, we were particularly interested in observing how teachers might respond to children of cultural backgrounds different from their own.

As in a previous study (Rubovits & Maehr, 1971), we arranged for students in an upper-level education class to participate in a micro-teaching experience. Such an exercise fit nicely with the goals of the course and seemed to be readily accepted by the students as a logical extension of in-class activities. As a matter of fact, it soon became obvious that the experience-starved students looked forward to this aspect of the course with a great deal of enthusiasm. In other words, there was absolutely no reason to believe that these prospective teachers suspected that they were doing anything other than participating in a standardized micro-teaching experience. They did not suspect that, in actuality, they were subjects in a teacher-expectancy study.

Before participating in the micro-teaching situation, the student teachers were given a lesson plan to follow. They were also told that some of their students were selected from the school's gifted program and some from regular classrooms in order to simulate a heterogeneously grouped classroom. Student teachers were further provided with detailed information about each child's ability and were encouraged to study this information thoroughly in order to prepare themselves for the teaching experience. As you may have surmised, the information was contrived for our purposes. The children were actually selected from the same tracks to assure that they would be of roughly the same ability. Whether a child was described as "gifted" or "average" was a matter of random assignment. Although we were interested in whether the student teachers would show favoritism in terms of the labels we assigned to the students, we were still more interested in any differential responses to black and white students. In each class, one "gifted" student and one "average" student were black, and one "gifted" student and one "average" student were white. All the teachers were white females, and, judging from our interview data, they were not bigoted but were certainly inexperienced with cultural diversity.

Admittedly, we did perpetrate a dirty trick on these unsuspecting teacher candidates. But the experiment yielded insights that were of value to them as well as to us. In view of what we all learned, the experimental deception was, I believe, fully justified. Some clearly prejudicial behavior patterns were revealed. In accord with the previously discussed Pygmalion research (Rubovits & Maehr, 1971), the student teachers responded more positively to "gifted" students than they did to "average" students. Generally, they acted in ways that would tend to fulfill the implicit prophecy of the labels—that is, *if* the student was white. Almost the opposite situation existed, however, when the student was black. Overall, blacks were treated less positively than whites, but what was most disturbing to all of us involved in this study was that it was the gifted black child who was discriminated against the most.

These results are indeed provocative. Perhaps *shocking* is a better word. Precisely because the results seem to be of such importance, a note of caution should be added. The study was done with teacher candidates in micro-teaching situations. Perhaps experienced teachers would have reacted differently, especially if they had interacted with the students over the course of a whole year. Perhaps not. There is limited evidence (Meichenbaum, Bowers, & Ross, 1969) that experienced teachers are no less susceptible to expectancy effects than inexperienced teachers and that interaction over a longer period of time does not necessarily rule out expectancy effects.

These findings and the results of other studies on the Pygmalion effect lead to an inevitable conclusion: teacher expectancy may result in teacher behavior that facilitates or inhibits the learning and development of the child. As true as that may be, it puts us in a peculiar dilemma at the conclusion of a book that has repeatedly emphasized that individuals must be understood in terms of culture, society, and group. Generalized knowledge of some sort seems to be a necessary preparation for teaching children of diverse cultural backgrounds. If we want to teach blacks in the inner city, whites in suburbia, or primitives in New Guinea, some prior knowledge about the life styles and thought patterns of these peoples is desirable. That same knowledge, however, can be used as little more than a collection of stereotypes about a people—stereotypes that create expectancies that may be far from correct in any individual case.

The Rubovits-Maehr results suggest a note of caution for those who have just read a book on the sociocultural origins of achievement and who are preparing to put this knowledge into practice. A little learning may be a dangerous thing. For example, there is the danger that, in writing this book, I have unwittingly caused some readers to discriminate against certain students, much as the student teachers did. It is impossible to refrain from categorizing in some way, and I have repeatedly found it necessary to use such labels as "disadvantaged children," "impoverished groups," "middle class," "Chicano," and a few others. A reader could—and some will—pick up only a label, a stereotype, or a prejudice. Such labels may create expectations that are inaccurate and unfortunate in any specific case. The seriousness of that possibility prompts a concluding caveat: generalized knowledge about cultures, societies, and people can harm as well as help.

Where does that leave us? Hopefully, there is a perspective implicit . in what has been said thus far that reduces the chances of harm and increases the possibilities of help. The teacher-expectancy studies contain an important but very specialized warning about the dangers of *limited* knowledge, but they certainly do not rule out the value of knowledge in itself. Knowledge of the child must be viewed as a kind of first step to effective teaching. It is probably just as important to know something about the child's sociocultural background as it is to know something about his level of reading. In both cases, a teacher ought to know more than a score on a test. Indeed, what the teacher really ought to know is how to learn about the child from the child. With regard to sociocultural origins, the teacher's knowledge of his or her students must consist of more than a stereotype— that is, more than an inflexible belief, idea, or theory. What he or she should know is that student and teacher alike are products of past as well as present social conditions. This book certainly has not provided a complete description of social backgrounds. Ideally, however, it has provided perspectives on the problem, forced the reader to ask a few questions on his own, and effectively persuaded him to remain open to new information—primarily to that information which he derives from the child.

There is another finding from the Pygmalion studies that may be of special interest. Although there is no strong reason to believe that experience alone will keep the teacher from operating in terms of group expectancies, not all teachers are equally dominated by such expectancies in dealing with an individual. Thus, one of the more interesting findings of the Rubovits-Maehr study was that the highly "dogmatic" teachers (Rokeach, 1960) showed the expectancy effects to a greater extent than the others did. Dogmatism is a personality trait that seems to be related to the degree to which individuals are open to new information and to which they operate in terms of this information rather than in terms of sets, particularly those given by authorities. Thus, not *all* teachers may be similarly susceptible to control by generalized expectancies. That is well to remember, and it does put a more optimistic slant on things. Conceivably, training teachers to overcome dogmatism—that is, to be flexible and open to new information—may diminish expectancy effects. The results of the Rubovits-Maehr study may also suggest that teacher training ought to focus more on the question of how to create such openness in teachers than on the question of how to provide teachers with appropriate materials and techniques.

Remaining open to new information—particularly to that information we derive from individual children—is important in all teaching. In teaching individuals with backgrounds different from our own, we must consider at least one other related point. There is a danger in stereotyping a group and in behaving inflexibly to a person in terms of such a stereotype. In addition, there is a danger that we may not recognize that educational institutions and methods are framed by a culture and inextricably entwined with it. In attempting to improve science teaching in developing countries, for example, there is a tendency simply to provide a direct translation of American curricular materials. Thus, if the Education Ministry of Sierra Leone wishes to develop scientists, it is often encouraged to consider and select one or another program sponsored by the U. S. National Science Foundation. The program is then translated into what is presumably the cultural idiom by an exchange of phrases and by the addition of a few culturally specific examples. A curriculum specialist who has worked extensively with this problem (Brown, in preparation) points out that, in spite of the materials, the teaching style actually does not change. While the American materials call for extensive student participation in experiments, the teacher in Sierra Leone may merely read aloud the contents of the laboratory manual to the class and may provide no chance for the student to engage in independent science making. Quite possibly, then, instead of merely imposing Western materials and teaching styles, we ought to assist developing countries in establishing their own curricula and pedagogy, urging them to look to their own culture for styles that are educationally feasible.

In any case, a teacher must be open to new information about and from the student and his culture. It is folly to assume that, since we know *something* about someone or some culture, we have learned all.

A QUESTION OF VALUE

Throughout this book, it is tacitly assumed that achievement is and should be a thing of value. In view of the typical commitments of American education, it is not surprising that such an assumption would be made. Yet, it might be well to take cognizance of an inevitable if bothersome question: "should achievement be all that important?" Although this is not a question that can be answered with any degree of confidence here, it is one that should be raised.

The importance of this question is perhaps most clearly evident when we consider the attempts to transport Western industrial styles, business procedures, and educational programs to a developing country. We have already raised questions about the *effectiveness* of imposing the achievement styles of one culture on another. Now we ask "should we even try to promote achievement?" In reading about the work of David McClelland, you may have questioned whether it was in fact right to create high-nAch persons in other societies. Shouldn't we "leave the natives alone"? In many ways, their life seems to be better than ours. Will our achievement styles bring them anything except ulcers, coronary thromboses, and the necessity for a psychiatric couch?

In all fairness to McClelland and his colleagues, it should be emphasized that they not only are aware of this "moral dilemma," but they also have struggled to work out an adequate solution (see McClelland & Winter, 1969, pp. 26 *ff.*, 366 *ff.*). They seem to have solved it to their own satisfaction by allowing the person who is seeking achievement training to make the value judgment. In other words, they have more or less assumed the role of nonjudgmental counselors. If the client decides that he wants to achieve certain ends, such as becoming achievement oriented, they will help him reach his goals. That, of course, merely represents a variant of the age-old approach of scholars and scientists to questions of value, ends, and purposes. It is also the approach of pragmatists in business and government. In spite of the fact that there are those who suggest that the approach is outmoded, it is not without its merit. Is it my business or anyone else's to tell the native of New Guinea that, in reality, his life is better than mine— that, although my way of life may bring him TV, autos, health clinics, and other things that he desires, his life is best? Is it not he who must make this decision?

Let's assume that the approach of letting the client decide is the fitting approach. There is still a clear responsibility for describing the alternatives to the clients as clearly as possible. It is obviously an error to stress that the Western achievement style has lead only to TV, autos, health clinics, and easy money; it also has led to pollution, family instability, and increased crime rates. McClelland and his colleagues have typically made a direct attempt to describe the negative consequences of achievement motivation in as detailed and accurate a fashion as possible. As a result, they have often lost a client who has decided that this was not for him. Yet, we probably do not know very much about what will really happen when we increase achievement in industry or in school. We know a great deal about some positive aspects, and we have a few stereotypes about the negative aspects. Clearly, the question for the future is "when a person is assisted in actualizing his achievement potential, what if anything is he forced to give up?" That is, what values must he sacrifice or what goals must he deemphasize?

That is a broad, global question with political and economic as well as educational overtones. There is a related but more specific question that may well be of more pressing interest to the educator or prospective teacher. If it is granted that, in some sense, achievement, the development of excellence, and progress in understanding and technology are necessary or desirable, is it the school's role to be primarily concerned with these issues? Among disadvantaged groups, there seems to be no question but that this is the school's business. The school is perhaps the only means through which achievement goals can be attained. For the American middle class, there are a variety of institutions, techniques, and possibilities available to assist the child in achieving and actualizing his intellectual potential. With increased availability of automated teaching devices, educational TV, and "enrichment programs," the child will have an ever-increasing possibility of achieving an accepted standard of competence without the aid of the school. In considering this situation, Coleman (1972) has suggested that schools might well devote an increased amount of their attention to the development of personal skills, such as social concern, personal responsibility, and altruism. Epigrammatically, schools might do well to focus less on the development of competence and more on the development of conscience. Though not without its problems, that is indeed an intriguing and thought-provoking suggestion.

A FINAL ANALYSIS

This book has had two focal points: the identification of an individual in a sociocultural context and the effects of this identification on achievement. Having repeatedly stressed the salience of these focal points,

I will conclude with a reminder that an exclusive and narrow concentration on either point is not without its limitations. This is not a cynical conclusion to an otherwise optimistic discourse. It is simply a tacit reminder that, when a person completes a learning experience, he should have not only more knowledge but also the insight necessary to ask better questions. Most emphatically, these questions do not relate solely to the quality of the knowledge base that has been presented or solely to the applicability of theory to practice; they also relate directly and immediately to the implications of that knowledge in determining the quality and direction of life. In short, it is not inappropriate to conclude by questioning the value of achievement after having been scientific and pragmatic. Although knowledge about educative processes is critical, knowledge about education inevitably culminates in questions of value. That is a fitting reminder with which to conclude a book that is largely dependent on scientific method but deeply concerned with the values, purposes, and beliefs of persons.

REFERENCES

Adkins, D. C., Payne, F. D., & Ballif, B. L. Motivational-factor scores for ten ethnic-cultural groups of preschool children. *American Educational Research Journal*, 1972, **9**, 557–572.

Allport, G. W., & Pettigrew, T. F. Cultural influence on the perception of movement: The trapezoidal illusion among Zulus. *Journal of Abnormal and Social Psychology*, 1957, **35**, 104–113.

Asch, S. E. *Social psychology*. Englewood Cliffs, N. J.: Prentice-Hall, 1952.

Asch, S. E. Effects of group pressure upon the modification and distortion of judgments. In E. E. Maccoby, T. M. Newcomb, & E. L. Hartley (Eds.), *Readings in social psychology*. New York: Holt, Rinehart & Winston, 1958.

Asher, S., & Allen, V. Racial preference and social comparison processes. *Journal of Social Issues*, 1969, **25**, 157–166.

Atkinson, J. W. (Ed.) *Motives in fantasy, action, and society*. Princeton, N. J.: Van Nostrand Reinhold, 1958.

Atkinson, J. W., & Feather, N. T. (Eds.) *A theory of achievement motivation*. New York: Wiley, 1966.

Baratz, S. B., & Baratz, J. C. Early childhood intervention: The social science base of institutional racism. *Harvard Educational Review*, 1970, **40**, 29–50.

Bartlett, F. C. *Remembering*. London: Cambridge University Press, 1932.

Bereiter, C. A nonpsychological approach to early compensatory education. In M. Deutsch, I. Katz, & A. R. Jensen (Eds.), *Social class, race, and psychological development*. New York: Holt, Rinehart & Winston, 1968.

Bereiter, C., & Engelmann, S. *Teaching disadvantaged children in the preschool*. Englewood Cliffs, N. J.: Prentice-Hall, 1966.

Bernstein, B. A sociolinguistic approach to socialization: With some reference to educability. In F. Williams (Ed.), *Language and poverty*. Chicago: Markham, 1970.

Birney, R. C. Research on the achievement motive. In E. F. Borgatta & W. W. Lambert (Eds.), *Handbook of personality theory and research*. Chicago: Rand McNally, 1968.

Boring, E. G. *A history of experimental psychology*. (2nd ed.) New York: Appleton-Century-Crofts, 1950.

Bronfenbrenner, U. *Two worlds of childhood: U. S. and U. S. S. R*. New York: Russell Sage Foundation, 1970.

Brown, R. *Social psychology*. New York: Free Press, 1965.

Brown, R. K. Thoughts on African science education. In M. L. Maehr & W. M.

Stallings (Eds.), *Culture, child, and school.* Monterey, Calif.: Brooks/Cole, in preparation.

Claiborne, W. L. Expectancy effects in the classroom: A failure to replicate. *Journal of Educational Psychology,* 1969, **60,** 377–383.

Clark, K. G., & Clark, M. P. Racial identification and preference in Negro children. In T. M. Newcomb & E. L. Hartley (Eds.), *Readings in social psychology.* New York: Holt, Rinehart & Winston, 1947. Pp. 169–178.

Coates, B. White adult behavior toward black and white children. *Child Development,* 1972, **43,** 143–154.

Cofer, C. N., & Appley, M. H. *Motivation: Theory and research.* New York: Wiley, 1964.

Cole, M. Culture and cognitive processes. In B. Maher (Ed.), *Introductory psychology.* New York: Wiley, 1972.

Cole, M., & Bruner, J. S. Cultural differences and inferences about psychological processes. *American Psychologist,* 1971, **26,** 867–876.

Coleman, J. S. *The adolescent society.* New York: Free Press, 1961.

Coleman, J. S. The children have outgrown the schools. *Psychology Today,* 1972, **5,** 72–75, 82.

Coleman, J. S., et al. *Equality of educational opportunity.* U. S. Department of Health, Education, and Welfare, Washington, D. C.: U. S. Government Printing Office, 1966.

Coles, R. It's the same, but it's different. *Daedalus,* 1965, **94,** 1107–1132.

Dawson, J. L. M. Psychological effects of social change in a West African community. Unpublished doctoral dissertation, University of Oxford, 1963.

deCharms, R. *Personal causation.* New York: Academic Press, 1968.

deCharms, R. Personal-causation training in schools. *Journal of Applied Social Psychology,* 1972, **2,** 95–113.

Deutsch, C. Auditory discrimination and learning social factors. *The Merrill-Palmer Quarterly,* 1964, **10,** 277–296.

Deutsch, C. Environment and perception. M. Deutsch, I. Katz, & A. R. Jensen (Eds.), *Social class, race, and psychological development.* New York: Holt, Rinehart & Winston, 1968.

Deutsch, M., & Brown, B. Social influences in Negro-white intelligence differences. *Journal of Social Issues,* 1964, **20**(2), 24–35.

Durkheim, E. *Suicide* (1897). (Trans. by J. A. Spaulding and G. Simpson.) New York: Free Press, 1958.

Eisenberg, L. Strengths of the inner-city child. In A. H. Passon, M. Goldberg, & A. J. Tannenbaum (Eds.), *Education of the disadvantaged.* New York: Holt, Rinehart & Winston, 1967.

Elashoff, J. D., & Snow, R. E. A case study in statistical inference: Reconsideration of the Rosenthal-Jacobson data on teacher expectancy. Technical report No. 15, Stanford Center for Research and Development in Teaching, Stanford University, Palo Alto, Calif., 1970.

Engelmann, S. How to construct effective language programs for the poverty child. In F. Williams (Ed.), *Language and poverty.* Chicago: Markham, 1970.

Finn, J. D. Expectations and the educational environment. *Review of Educational Research,* 1972, **42,** 387–410.

Flavell, J. H. *The developmental psychology of Jean Piaget.* Princeton, N. J.: Van Nostrand Reinhold, 1963.

French, E. G. Effects on interaction of motivation and feedback on task performance. In J. W. Atkinson (Ed.), *Motives in fantasy, action, and society*. Princeton, N. J.: Van Nostrand Reinhold, 1958.

Ginsburg, H., & Opper, S. *Piaget's theory of intellectual development*. Englewood Cliffs, N. J.: Prentice-Hall, 1969.

Goodenough, W. H. *Cooperation in change*. New York: Russell Sage Foundation, 1963.

Goodenough, W. H. *Culture, language, and society*. (A McCaleb Module in Anthropology.) Reading, Mass.: Addison-Wesley, 1971.

Goodman, K. S. Dialect barriers to reading comprehension. In J. C. Baratz & R. W. Shuy (Eds.), *Teaching black children to read*. Washington, D. C.: Center for Applied Linguistics, 1969.

Goodnow, J. A test of milieu differences with some of Piaget's tasks. *Psychological Monographs*, 1962, **76** (36, Whole No. 565).

Gottesman, I. I. Biogenetics of race and class. In M. Deutsch, I. Katz, & A. R. Jensen (Eds.), *Social class, race, and psychological development*. New York: Holt, Rinehart & Winston, 1968.

Greenfield, P. On culture and conservation. In J. S. Bruner, R. Oliver, P. Greenfield, et al. (Eds.), *Studies in cognitive growth*. New York: Wiley, 1966.

Greenfield, P., & Bruner, J. S. Culture and cognitive growth. In D. Goslin (Ed.), *Handbook of socialization theory and research*. Chicago: Rand McNally, 1969.

Gumperz, J. J., & Hernández-Chavez, E. Bilingualism, bidialectalism, and classroom interactions. In C. Cazden, V. John, & D. Hymes (Eds.), *Functions of language in the classroom*. New York: Teachers College Press, 1972.

Haas, H. I., & Maehr, M. L. Two experiments on the concept of self and the reaction of others. *Journal of Personality and Social Psychology*, 1965, **1**, 100–105.

Heckhausen, H. *The anatomy of achievement motivation*. New York: Academic Press, 1967.

Hess, R., & Shipman, V. Cognitive elements in maternal behavior. In J. P. Hill (Ed.), *Minnesota symposia on child psychology*. Vol. 1. Minneapolis: University of Minnesota Press, 1967. Pp. 57–81.

Horner, M. Sex differences in achievement motivation and performance in competitive and noncompetitive situations. (Doctoral dissertation, University of Michigan) Ann Arbor: University Microfilms, 1968, No. 69–12, 135.

Horner, M. The psychological significance of success in competitive achievement situations: A threat as well as a promise. In H. I. Day, D. E. Berlyne, & D. E. Hunt (Eds.), *Intrinsic motivation*. Toronto, Ont.: Holt, Rinehart & Winston, 1971.

Hudson, W. Pictorial depth perception in subcultural groups in Africa. *Journal of Social Psychology*, 1960, **52**, 183–208.

Hudson, W. Pictorial perception and educational adaptation in Africa. *Psychologia Africana*, 1962, **9**, 226–239.

Humphreys, L. Race and sex differences and their implications for educational and occupational equality. In M. L. Maehr & W. M. Stallings (Eds.), *Culture, child, and school*. Monterey, Calif.: Brooks/Cole, in preparation.

Hunt, D. E. *Matching models in education (Monograph Series No. 10)*. Toronto, Ont.: Ontario Institute for Studies in Education, 1971.

Hunt, J. McV. *The challenge of incompetence and poverty.* Urbana: University of Illinois Press, 1969.

Hunt, J. McV. Parent and child centers: Their basis in the behavioral and educational sciences. *American Journal of Orthopsychiatry,* 1971, **41,** 13–38.

Hunt, J. McV. Sequential order and plasticity in early psychological development. Paper presented at the Jean Piaget Society's Second Annual Symposium, Temple University, Philadelphia, Pa., May 1972.

Hunt, J. McV. Psychological assessment in education and social class. In M. L. Maehr & W. M. Stallings (Eds.), *Culture, child, and school.* Monterey, Calif.: Brooks/Cole, in preparation.

Hunt, J. McV., & Kirk, G. E. Social aspects of intelligence: Evidence and issues. In R. Cancro (Ed.), *Intelligence: Genetic and environmental influences.* New York: Grune & Stratton, 1971.

Jacobs, R. C., & Campbell, D. T. The perpetuation of an arbitrary tradition through several generations of a laboratory microculture. *Journal of Abnormal and Social Psychology,* 1961, **62,** 649–658.

Jencks, C., and various others. *Inequality: A reassessment of the effect of family and schooling in America.* New York: Basic Books, 1972.

Jensen, A. R. Social class and verbal learning. In M. Deutsch, I. Katz, & A. R. Jensen (Eds.), *Social class, race, and psychological development.* New York: Holt, Rinehart & Winston, 1968.

Jensen, A. R. How much can we boost IQ and scholastic achievement? *Harvard Educational Review,* 1969, **39,** 1–123.

John, V. P. Styles of learning—styles of teaching: Reflections on the education of Navajo children. In C. S. Cazden, V. P. John, & D. Hymes (Eds.), *Functions of language in the classroom.* New York: Teachers College Press, 1972.

Kamara, A., & Easley, J. A. Is the rate of cognitive development uniform across cultures? A methodological critique with new evidence from Themne children. In M. L. Maehr & W. M. Stallings (Eds.), *Culture, child, and school.* Monterey, Calif.: Brooks/Cole, in preparation.

Klinger, E., & McNelley, F. W. Fantasy-need achievement and performance: A role analysis. *Psychological Review,* 1969, **76,** 574–591.

Kluckhohn, F. Dominant and variant value orientations. In C. Kluckhohn and H. Murray (Eds.), *Personality in nature, culture, and society.* New York: Knopf, 1961.

Kluckhohn, F., & Strodtbeck, F. L. *Variations in value orientations.* Evanston, Ill.: Row, Peterson, 1961.

Kohlberg, L. Stage and sequence: The cognitive-developmental approach to socialization. In D. Goslin (Ed.), *Handbook of socialization theory and research.* Chicago: Rand McNally, 1969.

Kolb, D. A. Achievement-motivation training for underachieving high school boys. *Journal of Personality and Social Psychology,* 1965, **2,** 783–792.

Labov, W. The logic of nonstandard English. In F. Williams (Ed.), *Language and poverty.* Chicago: Markham, 1970.

Langer, T. S., & Michael, S. T. *Life stress and mental health.* New York: Free Press, 1963.

Lesser, G., Fifer, G., & Clark, D. Mental abilities of children in different social and cultural groups. In J. Roberts (Ed.), *School children in the urban slum.* New York: Free Press, 1967.

Lessing, E. E., & Zagorin, S. W. Black-power ideology and college students' attitudes toward their own and other racial groups. *Journal of Personality and Social Psychology,* 1972, **21,** 61–73. (a)

Lessing, E. E., & Zagorin, S. W. Black-power ideology and college students' attitudes toward their own and other racial groups: A correction. *Journal of Personality and Social Psychology,* 1972, **22,** 414–416. (b)

Lewis, O. *Children of Sanchez.* New York: Random House, 1961.

Liebow, E. *Tally's corner: A study of Negro street-corner men.* Boston: Little, Brown, 1967.

Ludwig, D. J., & Maehr, M. L. Changes in self-concept and stated behavioral preferences. *Child Development,* 1967, **38,** 453–467.

Maehr, M. L., Nafzger, S., & Mensing, J. Concept of self and the reaction of others. *Sociometry,* 1962, **25,** 353–357.

Maehr, M. L., & Sjogren, D. Atkinson's theory of achievement motivation: First step toward a theory of academic motivation? *Review of Educational Research,* 1971, **41,** 143–161.

Maehr, M. L., & Stallings, W. M. Freedom from external evaluation. *Child Development,* 1972, **43,** 177–185.

McClelland, D. C. *The achieving society.* New York: Free Press, 1961.

McClelland, D. C. Achievement motivation can be developed. *Harvard Business Review,* 1965, **43,** 6–24. (a)

McClelland, D. C. Toward a theory of motive acquisition. *American Psychologist,* 1965, 321–333. (b)

McClelland, D. C., Atkinson, J. W., Clark, R. A., & Lowell, E. L. *The achievement motive.* New York: Appleton-Century-Crofts, 1953.

McClelland, D. C., & Winter, D. G. *Motivating economic achievement.* New York: Free Press, 1969.

Mead, M. *Coming of age in Samoa.* New York: Morrow, 1928.

Meichenbaum, D. H., Bowers, K. S., & Ross, R. R. A behavioral analysis of teacher-expectancy effect. *Journal of Personality and Social Psychology,* 1969, **13,** 306–316.

Menz, F. Disconfirmation and performance on a verbal-achievement task. Unpublished doctoral dissertation, University of Illinois, 1970.

Miller, G. A., & McNeill, D. Psycholinguistics. In G. Lindzey & E. Aronson (Eds.), *The handbook of social psychology.* Vol. 3. Reading, Mass.: Addison-Wesley, 1968.

Milner, E. A study of the relationship between reading readiness in grade one schoolchildren and patterns of parent-child interaction. *Child Development,* 1951, **22,** 95–112.

Minor, M. W. Experimenter-expectancy effect as a function of evaluation apprehension. *Journal of Personality and Social Psychology,* 1970, **15,** 326–332.

Mosteller, F., & Moynihan, D. (Eds.) *On equality of educational opportunity.* New York: Vintage (Random House), 1972.

Mundy-Castle, A. C. Pictorial depth perception in Ghanaian children. *International Journal of Psychology,* 1966, **1,** 290–300.

Mundy-Castle, A. C., & Nelson, G. K. A neuropsychological study of the Knysna forest workers. *Psychologia Africana,* 1962, **9,** 240–272.

O'Connor, P., Atkinson, J. W., & Horner, M. Motivational implications of ability grouping in schools. In J. W. Atkinson & N. T. Feather (Eds.), *A theory of achievement motivation.* New York: Wiley, 1966.

Pettigrew, T. Social-evaluation theory: Convergences and applications. In D.

Levine (Ed.), *Nebraska symposium on motivation, 1967*. Lincoln: University of Nebraska Press, 1967.

Phillips, J. L. *The origins of intellect: Piaget's theory*. San Francisco: Freeman, 1969.

Proshansky, H. M., & Newton, P. The nature and meaning of Negro self-identity. In M. Deutsch, I. Katz, & A. R. Jensen (Eds.), *Social class, race, and psychological development*. New York: Holt, Rinehart & Winston, 1968.

Rainwater, L. Crucible of identity: The Negro lower-class family. *Daedalus*, 1966, **95**, 172–217.

Rokeach, M. *The open and closed mind*. New York: Basic Books, 1960.

Rokeach, M. *Beliefs, attitudes, and values*. San Francisco: Jossey-Bass, 1968.

Rosen, B. C. Race, ethnicity, and the achievement syndrome. *American Sociological Review*, 1959, **24**, 47–60.

Rosen, B. C. Socialization and achievement motivation in Brazil. *American Sociological Review*, 1962, **27**, 612–624.

Rosenthal, R. *Experimenter effects in behavioral research*. New York: Appleton-Century-Crofts, 1966.

Rosenthal, R., & Jacobson, L. *Pygmalion in the classroom: Teacher expectation and pupils' intellectual development*. New York: Holt, Rinehart & Winston, 1968.

Rubovits, P. C. Early experience and the socialization of achieving orientations. In M. L. Maehr & W. M. Stallings (Eds.), *Culture, child, and school*. Monterey, Calif.: Brooks/Cole, in preparation.

Rubovits, P. C., & Maehr, M. L. Pygmalion analyzed: Toward an explanation of the Rosenthal-Jacobson findings. *Journal of Personality and Social Psychology*, 1971, **19**, 197–203.

Rubovits, P. C., & Maehr, M. L. Pygmalion black and white. *Journal of Personality and Social Psychology*, 1973, **25**, 210–218.

Rubovits, P. C., & Maehr, M. L. Teacher expectations: A special problem for black children with white teachers. In M. L. Maehr & W. M. Stallings (Eds.), *Culture, child, and school*. Monterey, Calif.: Brooks/Cole, in preparation.

Schafer, W. E., & Olexa, C. *Tracking and opportunity*. Scranton, Pa.: Chandler, 1971.

Schneider, L., & Lysgaard, S. The deferred-gratification pattern: A preliminary study. *American Sociological Review*, 1953, **18**, 142–149.

Segall, M., Campbell, D. T., & Herskovits, M. J. *The influence of culture on visual perception*. Indianapolis: Bobbs-Merrill, 1966.

Sherif, M. A study of some social factors in perception. *Archives of Psychology*, 1935, No. 187.

Sherif, M. *The psychology of social norms*. New York: Harper & Row, 1936.

Shuy, R. W. A linguistic background for developing reading materials for black children. In J. C. Baratz & R. W. Shuy (Eds.), *Teaching black children to read*. Washington, D.C.: Center for Applied Linguistics, 1969.

Sigel, I. Language of the disadvantaged: The distancing hypothesis. In C. B. Lavatelli (Ed.), *Promising practices in language development*. Urbana: University of Illinois Press, 1970.

Smith, C. P. Conclusion. In C. P. Smith (Ed.), *Achievement-related motives in children*. New York: Russell Sage Foundation, 1969.

Snow, R. E. Unfinished Pygmalion. *Contemporary Psychology*, 1969, **14**, 197–199.

Stodolsky, S. S., & Lesser, G. Learning patterns in the disadvantaged. *Harvard Educational Review,* 1967, **37,** 546–593.

Strodtbeck, F. L. Family interaction, values, and achievement. In D. C. McClelland et al. (Eds.), *Talent and society.* Princeton, N.J.: Van Nostrand Reinhold, 1958, 135–194.

Stuempfig, D. W., & Maehr, M. L. Persistence as a function of conceptual structure and quality of feedback. *Child Development,* 1970, **41,** 1183–1190.

Terrell, G., Durkin, K., & Wiesley, M. Social class and the nature of the incentive in discrimination learning. *Journal of Abnormal and Social Psychology,* 1959, **59,** 270–272.

Thomas, W. I. *Primitive behavior: An introduction.* New York: McGraw-Hill, 1937.

Thorndike, R. L. Review of *Pygmalion in the classroom. American Educational Research Journal,* 1968, **5,** 708–711.

Thorndike, R. L. But do you have to know how to tell time? *American Educational Research Journal,* 1969, **6,** 692.

Thornes, R. Differential effects of the origin-pawn dimension on intrinsic need-achievement. Unpublished doctoral dissertation, University of Illinois, 1971.

Valentine, C. A. *Culture and poverty: Critique and counterproposal.* Chicago: University of Chicago Press, 1968.

Vernon, P. E. Environmental handicaps and intellectual developments: Parts I and II. *British Journal of Educational Psychology,* 1965, **35,** 117–126.

Weber, M. *The Protestant ethic and the spirit of capitalism.* (First Ed., 1904.) (Trans. by T. Parsons.) New York: Scribner, 1930.

Weiner, B. Implications of the current theory of achievement motivation for research and performance in the classroom. *Psychology in the Schools,* 1967, **4,** 164–171.

Weiner, B. New conceptions in the study of achievement motivation. In B. Maher (Ed.), *Progress in experimental personality research.* Vol. 5. New York: Academic Press, 1970.

Weiner, B. *Theories of motivation.* Chicago: Markham, 1972.

White, B. L. An experimental approach to the effects of experience on early human development. In J. P. Hill (Ed.), *Minnesota Symposia on Child Psychology.* Vol. 1. Minneapolis: University of Minnesota Press, 1967. Pp. 201–226.

White, B. L., Castle, O., & Held, R. Observations on the development of visually-directed reaching. *Child Development,* 1964, **35,** 349–364.

White, B. L., & Held, R. Plasticity of sensorimotor development in the human infant. In J. F. Rosenblith & W. Allinsmith (Eds.), *The causes of behavior: Readings in child development and educational psychology* (2nd ed.) Boston: Allyn and Bacon, 1966.

White, R., & Lippitt, R. Leader behavior and member reaction in three "social climates." In D. Cartwright & A. Zander (Eds.), *Group Dynamics.* (3rd ed.) New York: Harper & Row, 1968.

Whorf, B. L. Science and linguistics. *Technology Review,* 1940, **44,** 229–248.

Whorf, B. L. *Language, thought, and reality.* (Ed. by J. B. Carroll.) Cambridge: MIT Press and New York: Wiley, 1956.

Winterbottom, M. R. The relation of childhood training in independence to achievement motivation. Unpublished doctoral dissertation, University of Michigan, 1953.

Winterbottom, M. R. The relation of need for achievement to learning experiences in independence and mastery. In J. W. Atkinson (Ed.), *Motives in fantasy, action, and society*. Princeton, N. J.: Van Nostrand Reinhold, 1958. Pp. 453–478.

Zander, A., & Forward, J. Position in group, achievement motivation, and group aspirations. *Journal of Personality and Social Psychology*, 1968, **8**, 282–288.

Zigler, E. Social class and the socialization process. *Review of Educational Research*, 1970, **40**, 87–110.

Zigler, E., & Kanzer, P. The effectiveness of two classes of verbal reinforcers on the performance of middle- and lower-class children. *Journal of Personality*, 1962, **30**, 157–163.

INDEX